WHY DOES THE
WEST FORGET?

SPIRE

Emma Nicholson

WHY DOES
THE WEST FORGET?

Spire is an imprint of Hodder & Stoughton *Publishers*

British Library Cataloguing in Publication Data

A catalogue record for this title is
available from the British Library

ISBN 0-340-60021-7

*Published by Hodder and Stoughton, a division of Hodder and Stoughton
Ltd, Mill Road, Dunton Green, Sevenoaks, Kent TN13 2YA Editorial Office:
47 Bedford Square, London WC1B 3DP*

*Typeset by Hewer Text Composition Services, Edinburgh. Printed in Great
Britain by Cox & Wyman Ltd.*

This book is dedicated to Ayatollah Al-Hakim in honour and recognition of his leadership in the fight between good and evil

Life
is only
for
Love

Time
is only that
we may find
God

FOREWORD BY THE
RT. HON. DOUGLAS HURD, CBE, MP

Emma Nicholson has given the world an inspiring example in her work to draw attention to the repression of
the marsh Arabs of Southern Iraq and to bring them
humanitarian relief. In *Why Does the West Forget?* she
describes a life which has been dedicated to the service
of others, beginning with her work in the development
field in India. This background informs her commitment to countering repression in Iraq, on which she
has assembled convincing case histories of systematic
abuse of human rights by the Baghdad regime. In the
two years in which Emma and I have worked together
to help these brave people I have been impressed by
her courage and her commitment. Her moving account
of how she first became involved with the marsh Arabs
and of how the Amar appeal was launched will bring her
work to a wider audience. She deserves and has our full
support.

Illustration Acknowledgements

All photographs used by kind permission.

Shustar camp, makeshift classroom, widower, camp child, and childhood joy: © Vahid Farmand.

Inside the marshes, Napalm bomb victim, Basra mine victim: © Bob Collier

Iraqi Shi'ites on Iranian border × 3: © Tony Smith

Sheik Hammoodi with Archbishop Carey: © Terry Moore

Amar: © John Lyne

Contents

Acknowledgements

Much of this book is devoted to the plight of the Iraqi victims of recent and ongoing oppression in their own country. Many new groups and individuals have come forward to help whose work should be recognised and honoured. I note a small number below.

The Trustees of the Amar Appeal are: Bill Dodds, Gareth Griffiths, Lord Jellicoe, Professor David Morley, Sir Anthony Parsons, Betty Pelekanos, Mike Regan, Anthony Rowsell (Vice-Chairman), Ernest Williams, and myself as Chairman. Our Secretary is Jeanette Sidey.

Others who have helped Amar himself include his surgeons and medical advisers, John Clarke, David Gateley and staff in Rothschild Ward of Guy's Hospital; deputy head-teacher Dr Al-Hasani, tutor Dr T. Hashim and Principal Mike Fielding; Veronica Carter of the Official Solicitor's Office, Jeanne Kaniuk and Lorna Zumpe of the Thomas Coram organisation, Devon bank manager Roger Brown and Joan and Jim Lewington.

The Amar Appeal has a sister organisation, the Iraqi Humanitarian Relief Committee. Dr Hamid Al-Bayati is Vice-Chairman, other members include Rashid Rumani, Dr Abdul Karim Habib, Dr Sundis Bahia, Munya Allawi, and I am the Chairman. This group was founded by Dr Amir Al-Tabatabaie, Hazim Mahdi and Abo Haydar Zewin.

Iraqi friends in the West whose help has been outstand-

ing include Dr M. Haydar Hassan and his two brothers,
Mohammed and Ali; Yousif Al-Khoei, Laith Kubba and
others in the Al-Khoei foundation; Dr Al-Bayati and
his colleagues in the SCIRI offices worldwide and Dr
S. Bahrul-Uloom and his family. Other key players are
Dr Sahib Al-Hakim, the London representative of Human
Rights in Iraq, and all the members of the Iraqi Women's
Association, in particular their Chairman and Secretary,
Aidi Ossierman and Dr K. Al-Saidi, whose support is
constant.

Dr Ahmed Chalabi, Chairman of the Executive Committee Iraqi National Congress, who co-ordinates the
work they are doing to pull together the opposition
groups. Sheik Hamoodi now leads their International
Humanitarian wing. Umar Hegedus of AMANA has
enlarged my knowledge of Islam as has, of course, the
General Secretary of the Islamic Council and my old
friend Salem Azzam. Dr Chibli Mallatt of the School of
Oriental and African Studies is a true professional in the
field of Islamic law.

Major Peter Westmacott, former Deputy Private
Secretary to HRH The Prince of Wales, showed immense
understanding. The Prince himself gave us a thoughtful
and wide-ranging introductory letter for the Amar Appeal
leaflet. A unique endorsement of humanitarian needs,
irrespective of ways of worship, was given by the Bishop
of Crediton, Peter Coleman, Rabbi Julian Jacobs and
Ayatollah Mousawi at the official launch of the Amar
Appeal call for funds.

Throughout the past two years the officials and Min-
isters of the Foreign and Commonwealth Office of Her
Majesty's Government have given insight and support.
Douglas Hurd, the Foreign Secretary, has listened constantly; Douglas Hogg and Mark Lennox-Boyd have
responded in the House to Parliamentary Questions and
debates. Patrick Nixon and his staff, including Frances
Guy, have always helped. Ambassadors David Reddaway
and David Gore-Booth have been outstandingly helpful

and welcoming. Baroness Lynda Chalker, Dr David Nabarro and Mary McCowan of the Overseas Development Administration have been assiduous in their help for the Iraqi victims, both north and south.

The Ambassador for Saudi Arabia to the UK, his Excellency Ghazi Algosaibi, and the former Ambassador for the State of Kuwait, Ghazi Al-Reyes, gave generously both personally and from their governments to help the humanitarian work.

Vladimir Ivanov of the Embassy of the Russian Federation found the two best surgeons for our Tehran medical mission from Moscow.

On the initiative of the Amar Appeal, the International Union for the Conservation of Nature (IUCN) recently agreed to review a major and far-reaching survey of the report on the Wetlands of southern Iraq and Iran by Exeter University. The introduction to the scientists came from Dr David Harrison whom I approached in his capacity as Chairman of the Committee of Vice-Chancellors. Dr Edward Maltby, reader in geography there and Chairman of the Wetlands Committee of the IUCN came forward at once and took up the challenge. Both Dr Harrison and Dr Maltby deserve warm thanks.

HRH The Prince Philip gave a crucial introduction to Dr Claude Martin of the World Wildlife Fund, who helped forward the IUCN decision.

The European Commission Humanitarian Office (ECHO) have been superb in their continuing understanding and support financially. Mr Richard Lewartowski and his colleague Mr Tony Watkins-Burton merit very special thanks. Members of the European Parliament have constantly put forward motions in support of the Iraqi victims, led by British MEPs Lord Plumb, Christopher Prout, and Edward McMillan-Scott. The UK Ambassador in Geneva, Martin Moreland, and Ali-Adadh of SCIRI in Geneva both helped in different ways.

Max Van der Stoel, and before him Prince Sadruddin Aga Khan, assisted by John Packer, are tireless in their search

for human rights in Iraq. Gerard Putman-Cramer, Chief of
the UN Department of the Humanitarian Affairs Special
Unit in Iraq, is a true professional also. Dr Nicholas Ward
of the World Health Organisation in Geneva responded
rapidly to requests for help with his natural generosity.

At the United Nations headquarters in New York, Jan
Eliasson, Deputy Secretary General for Humanitarian
Affairs in the United Nations, and Henry Breed, formerly
of the Iraq Office, and other staff there, give all the help
they can, as do the UK Mission for the United Nations. On
the voluntary network, US citizens Gay Schoene and Cary
Stratton-Boyd set up a wonderful appeal in Newburyport,
Massachusetts.

Rend Rahim Francke and Dr Mahdi Al-Bassam of the
Iraq Foundation, USA, have become friends too. Senator
Edward Kennedy and Peter Galbraith of the Senate Staff
Committee on Foreign Relations gave time to think on the
plight of Iraq, as did Ambassador Bill Dyess, a real friend
to those in trouble world-wide.

Iraqi refugee friends in Iran are large in number and
headed by Ayatollah Mohamad Baqir Al-Hakim, to whom
this book is dedicated. The Iraqi Humanitarian Relief
Food Aid Committee in Tehran has been chaired by
Dr Abu Ahmed Ramadan. The Amar Appeal Tehran
Medical Committee, bringing aid to help the Iraqi refu-
gees within Iran includes the following health or welfare
professionals: Dr Sahib Al-Hariri (Iranian-Iraqi doctor,
Chairman); Dr M.B. Shahedi-Ferd (Iranian doctor); Qusim
Hussain Haidari (Iraqi senior accountant); Dr Dilshad
(senior Iranian doctor and a former Minister of Health);
Vahid Farmand (representative of Ministry of Foreign
Affairs); Hussan Shoshteri-Zada (representative of Health
Department, Deputy Chairman of Iranian Red Crescent).
The Amar Appeal Medical Committee in Ahwāz, who work
directly with the refugees include: Dr Zuhair Mosawi (Iraqi
doctor); Dr Ameen Asadin (senior Iraqi doctor with MRCP
degree); Dr Nick Khouh (General Director of Health in
Khozestaan); Dr Monbini (Head of Ahwāz University); Dr

Dibaee (Deputy General Director, Head of Forensic Department); and Abdil-Nubi Gatia (Deputy Director of Foreign Affairs in Khozestaan Governorate). The international team of surgeons who operated in Tehran as volunteers was made up of Anthony Rowsell, John Clarke and David Gateley of Guy's and St. Thomas' Hospital in London, together with Georgy Borisovich Yakolev and Alexei Yurievich Yashin of Moscow's leading Burns Unit.

I have many new Iranian friends who work with me to bring aid to the refugee camps in a voluntary capacity outside their professional duties. They include: Aga Mohamadi, now patron of the Amar appeal, who works to the President, Mr Vahid Farmand, First Assistant to the Persian Gulf Department, Mr Ajouni, Second Assistant and Sayeid Zahedi, Third Assistant, Dr Hamid Reza Assefi, Director West of Europe and Foumani Haeri, Adviser to the Minister and General Director, all from the Ministry of Foreign Affairs. Mr Kharegani and Gholamreza Ansari, chargés d'affaires in the Iranian Mission to the UK, Deputy Head of Mission Mohammed Safei and their colleagues in the Iranian Embassies in London and New York are always hospitable and helpful. Media friends are now many and varied.

Jeanette Sidey and Ruth Manning head a list of staff volunteers who have helped in so many ways. David Lindsay and Jerome Le-Roy (Iraqi refugees), Christopher Gillibrand (Romanian orphans), Chris Stott, Ralph Wilkinson, Hazel Clarke and others are generous and skilful with professional help, as are David McCluney, Nick Crocker, Paul Haerle and Jim Holland, all former IBM senior project managers, and many others.

The Archbishop of Canterbury has pledged his full support.

James Catford of Hodder and Stoughton inspired this book.

Michael Caine, my husband, and Amar give me space, encouragement and fun always.

Introduction

It hasn't been easy to get inside the marshes of Iraq since the Gulf War ended in March 1991, nor to visit the hostels for the Iraqi wounded in Tehran or Ahwāz (a dusty Iranian border town). It's hard to get permission to enter refugee camps of the Iraqi Shi'ites or talk with those now squatting on the borders of Iran. In the wake of the eight-year horror of the Iran–Iraq War security is very tight on the Iranian side. But only there is it possible to see the weight of cruelty that Saddam Hussein has inflicted on the Iraqi Shi'ites since he took power in the long years following 1979.

Look there at the deformed bodies of his torture victims, see the disfigured face and bleeding wounds of a napalm-bombed boy, listen to the words of men, women and children with their grim stories of unending torment and death. You reach just one conclusion: that the Baghdad regime has set out to obliterate the southern Shi'ites as well as the Kurds in the north. Their evil mission has been to search out and destroy those who are the most educated and thoughtful people of modern Iraq, those who can build a society and make it function. The university professors and schoolteachers, the doctors and chemists, the businessmen and oil experts, shopkeepers, taxi-drivers and farmers; these are the victims, the targets of Saddam's unquenchable hatred.

The campaign by Saddam Hussein against the nation's

Shi'ites long pre-dates the Gulf War. For the first evidence of a Hitler-like repression of the south was there as far back as 1977 in frequent official attacks on people and property, arrests and imprisonments, tortures and deaths.

That year the young brother of a surgeon friend of mine, aged fourteen years, was seized and imprisoned with constant torture for eleven years. Daily he was strung up by one leg from the ceiling and used as the butt of the guards' cruelty. A brother of another friend of mine, aged seventeen, was hung on a large electric fan in front of his mother. The battering of the fan killed him; she died of shock. A young and brilliant research chemist, with an intellect that few possess, was dragged into the streets and beaten to death. His crime? Just like countless other victims, and millions still to suffer, he was a Shi'ite.

The early written orders from Saddam Hussein and others like him to their southern-based Army generals stretch back fifteen years. They are chilling in the finality of their execution plans for Shi'ites. The curt statements carry no justification for the orders of destruction of a man, a family, a street of homes, a village. The words used – 'destroy', 'obliterate', 'kill' – are surely evidence for a Nuremberg-type trial.

Thousands have been confined in prisons where torture is remorseless and unremitting, hundreds of thousands of men, women and children have been killed, the same number again have fled to the safe haven of Iran, and half a million starving and disease-ridden people are now struggling for survival in the bleak marshes formed by the historic Tigris and Euphrates rivers.

Countless case-files of victims and other documentation can be found now in Tehran in the office of the Documental Centre for Human Rights in Iraq. Late in 1991, I met with a group of victims in my search for new evidence with which to convince the Allies of the continual Shi'ite genocide and the need for military protection for the marsh Arabs. Among the victims there was a surgeon who had recently escaped from Iraq through the marshes. A few years earlier he had been seized and tortured mercilessly, day after day, with breaks for him to recover consciousness. He had fled the gaol with many other prisoners in the wake of a successful Allied Forces' bombing raid during the Gulf War, and slowly made his way secretly out of Iraq and into the safe haven of Iran. I needed an interpreter to accompany me into the Iraqi marshes. Without hesitation he agreed to my request and came back into Iraq with me, accepting the risks, working under fire and sailing within a mile of Saddam's Republican Guard front-line troops in battle.

The evidence I found there and in the refugee camps showed that Saddam Hussein has been determined to destroy not just homes and families but their culture too. Educational provision in the south of Iraq has been minimal for years now. Children are growing up illiterate and non-numerate as – despite the efforts of their own parents and spiritual leaders – without books, teaching equipment, salaries for teachers or even schools, no real education can take place. Thousands of children in the refugee camps in southern Iran are struggling to learn the basic skills of reading, writing and maths. In the camps there are refugee teachers but there are virtually no books; one camp of 3000 refugees has thirty-five books, of which only one is in Arabic. The teachers try to keep the children's attention in a concrete shed with a corrugated iron roof, teaching in temperatures of over 40°C.

Some of Iraq's holiest cities, with thousands of years of religious history and of incomparable beauty architecturally have been destroyed. Ordinary people are forbidden to worship. Hundreds of holy men have been executed, and others have fled.

In the depths of the marshes the situation is worse with no medicines and little food, save for the small amounts smuggled in by boat through Iran. That slender route has become more difficult to use in recent months as the Iraqi military net around the marshes has tightened remorselessly. The vast, historic waterways are bedded with dense forests of shifting papyrus reeds stretching two or three times the height of a man. The static water, dense with suspended particles of sludge, stinks of rotting vegetation and excrement. The heavy air is thick with malarial mosquitoes, the temperature over 50°C and sunstroke is common. Only the marsh Arabs, the Ma'dan, whose history stretches back to 6000 BC, have managed to exist in this environment so hostile to human life.

Bomb craters and large, burnt reed beds (to smoke out the Shi'ites) mark the assaults. Continuing gunfire sounds along the border on the Iraqi side. The shallower exit lanes are choked with military obstacles – rusting tanks, mounted guns on concrete emplacements, barbed-wire barricades – designed to stop the refugees' small boats so that they can be caught and killed. Even within the marshes there is no sanctuary. Where there was once water, now cracked mud beds give no support to traditional rice-farming, fish or water-buffalo. Saddam Hussein's water engineers spent summer and autumn 1992 damming and diverting the waterways, and the work was nearly complete in summer 1992.

Polluted water is now all that there is to drink. Without a place to deposit sewage, either human or animal, most of those now in the marshes suffer constant dysentery. There is no cold chain of refrigeration to get the vaccines in, so there are no vaccines in the marshes and children cannot be immunised. Polio, measles, whooping cough, mumps and other childhood diseases are rampant. The children are stunted as breast milk is in short supply because of severe maternal malnutrition. Without even the most primitive obstetric services, mothers are dying in labour. Pre-natal protein deficiency impacts on children's brain development in the womb.

In 1991 the Allies had completed a famous victory. Fighting under the United Nations banner, Western and Arab forces drove the arch-monster, Saddam Hussein, right out of tiny Kuwait, restoring precious reserves of oil to Kuwait's Western-friendly rule. In their haste to complete a peace treaty just past the hundred days since war was started, the Allied generals forgot to take the Kuwait border map showing the mined areas from their Iraqi counterparts. This caused large trouble eighteen months on, when UN border guards could not give chase as British, Swedish and Kuwaiti nationals were taken hostage and placed in Baghdad's Abu Ghaireb prison, to be used as bargaining counters in the sanctions game.

Another error was to believe the Iraqi losers in their stated desire to use army helicopters for mercy missions on internal flights, presented as food-aid transporters. Those same helicopters, retained by the Iraq Air Force courtesy of the USA peacemakers, were gun-mounted and subsequently used against their own people – until the Allied adoption of the southern Iraq no-fly zone in August 1992 – to machine-gun and drop chemical weapons on Iraqi citizens who oppose Saddam's continuing reign of terror. For at the end of the Gulf War, tempted to dash for internal freedom by George Bush's radio messages and leaflet-drops apparently offering logistical support, the Kurds rose up in the north of Iraq and the Shi'ites in the south. George Bush's messages proved worthless, and death and destruction followed. On our television screens the West saw and reacted to the Kurdish tragedy. We did not see what happened in the south, where, subsequently, wave upon wave of military assaults on civilian towns and villages, farms and communities have been carried out on the orders of Saddam Hussein and his commanders.

I have been able to see some of the tragedy through the humanitarian welcome of the Iranian Government and people. I've visited and brought in aid (food, clothing and medicines from world-wide donors) to camp refugees, border squatters and marsh people. The friendship of Iran to the partnership of the Iraqi Opposition has made this work achievable.

But the situation worsens daily. I travelled on one

trip through marshes smoking from ground-launched
bombardments, from missiles and tank cannon. One
missile barrage had landed perhaps an hour before I
reached the place. It left behind a charred, devastated
area of about 300 metres. The effect of such hits on the
marsh-dwellers' tight-packed, reed-built villages is easy
to see. Hundreds of such villages have been razed and
their small rice plots burned.

Many refugees have made the dangerous dash across
the border into Iran. But to make the crossing, they must
brave mined waters and an army of Saddam's soldiers
deployed to thwart their escape. On another trip, my
small boat passed through a stretch of water 'cleared'
of mines at the cost of families who had tried to flee by
that route a week earlier. Several hundred people (men,
women and children) had been blown to death. Some will
not fully leave the marshes because their water buffalo,
the only asset they have, cannot survive on the dry
ground of the Iranian side. Ten thousand men, women
and children squat there now, without tents, mats, food
or water to hand.

Just towards the end of my trip in August 1992,
entirely by chance, I encountered on the Iranian border
a family group I'd met once before, in August 1991.
The deterioration in their condition was pitiable. Barely
alive, they couldn't manage the forty-kilometre trip to a
food and clothing centre my team had set up. Yet they
welcomed me again as a witness and sharer of their
despair. The grandmother said the children ran to me
because I brought them the smell of Iraq, their home.
She told me again of the murders she had witnessed – her
husband, brothers, sons and uncles. She had been forced
by Saddam's troops to stand close during their executions
after the failed uprising. Her nostrils, she said, still reek
of blood. She fled with the other women, children and
elders to the sanctuary of the Iranian borders.

The old woman's aba – the black cloak Shi'ite women
wear to shield their modesty – had worn threadbare in

the year since I'd first met her. I handed her my own, still heavy with mud from the marshes that had been her home, and she walked tall once more with the renewal of her dignity.

Her world in those marshes stretches back for thousands of years. It is in these lands, between the Tigris and Euphrates rivers, that Western civilisation began with Sumeria, Akkadia and Babylon. It is our history, too, that is being destroyed. And yet, we have forgotten or chosen to ignore their suffering. Why does the West forget?

1

Christian Heritage

I was born into a Christian culture whose literary, musical and visual richness, stretching back over a thousand years, made up the tapestry of our world.

Our lives as children were comforting and secure. Myself and my three sisters went to Sunday School each week. Our travelling nursery school came to us or, for a different term, we went to a nearby farmhouse. Our values were fixed and our rebellions (my own by far the most frequent) were against the buttresses of known certainties. The Christian year erected the milestones against which we checked our progress. Fasting in purple Lent (no meat on Friday) led to the black-cloaked pains of Holy Week and the gold-white triumph of Easter Day. The imponderable wonder of Whitsuntide was followed by the long, green Trinity season. Advent began at the foot of the mountain that we climbed to reach the Bethlehem Star of Christmas. Christmas had its own excitement, like a bubble that never burst. Like all the Christian festivals, it started the night before (we were taught that the Christian day begins at 6 p.m. and ends a twenty-four hour period later).

My mother began our Christmases by reading Clement Moore's Christmas poem. On other evenings we lay upstairs in bed awaiting, if we were lucky, her measured steps coming up the creaky stairs of our old house to read to us. Bedtimes were fixed but fought against.

They always seemed too early and in the long summer months it was a particular burden to keep quiet and pretend to sleep while daylight still streamed in through unlined curtains. But Christmas Eve was different, we were allowed downstairs. My mother's calm and deep voice, containing as it so often did a *frisson* of unnamed excitement began: 'The night before Christmas, when nothing was stirring, not even a mouse.' She read as we huddled comfortably up against her large armchair, which faced my father's smaller one on the other side of the flickering fire. He set aside his chess board and picked up his snuff box to listen too. But it was the pictures in the book that created Christmas for me most powerfully, the Arthur Rackham illustrations of Father Christmas, red-robed and merry, smiling his way into the houses of loving families and vanishing, having left his good things, without trace. Even his reindeer were named and were known as individuals with their quirks and naughtinesses just like our ponies in the field. His sleigh was a grander, grown-up version of the toboggans made of wood without runners on which we careered downhill in icy snow in the woods or on crunchy gravel and puddles on the road.

Somehow, and somewhat inexplicably, Father Christmas was also St Nicholas. As in all the best mysteries there was a confusion of identity and purpose, giving an uncertain twist to the Christmas story. Father Christmas came to see each child everywhere on Christmas Eve and celebrated winter. St Nicholas visited only Dutch children, some three weeks earlier on 6 December, to mark the birth of Christ. It was a little like the intertwining of the Christian calendars, whereby the Orthodox Church celebrated Easter at a different time to Western Christianity. St Nicholas filled clogs not stockings, and I imagine that he skated too, as did those swirling figures in Dutch paintings. At the time, it did not matter to us that on Christmas Eve the two figures became one, the pagan symbol and the Christian saint, and as we sat by the wood fire, with logs placed carefully in their proper places by my father so that the flames kept rising, our excitement rose. Later that night we were honour-bound to go to sleep so that Father Christmas could come and visit us once eyes were closed and lights were off.

Early in the morning, the first sensation of awakening was the heavy pressure on my feet and the sound of thumps and rustles if other sisters were awake beforehand. Our bedrooms were cold on Christmas morning since we dared not light our coal bedroom fires the evening before or have them lit for us in case, coming down the chimney, Father Christmas might burn his feet. Frost on our bedroom windows and, if we were indeed lucky, snow on the window-sills gave a perfection to the coming day. Once we had opened our Christmas stockings (my father's shooting stockings), filled up and bursting with small presents, each wrapped in different-coloured crêpe paper and tied up with wool we put on best dresses and came down to breakfast.

From the safety of our Sunday School class here were the securities of a stable Christian community. Peter Hiscock – our farm manager and gardener, our childhood friend – rang the church bells with others, in harsh medieval harmony, calling in the congregation, many of whom on this festival day had unknown faces but familiar features. They were introduced later as visiting brothers, sisters or aunts of the families from the village or outlying farms. On ordinary Sundays the numbers resumed their normal strength. In the pew on the other side of the narrow aisle were the Hurd family. Anthony Hurd, the Newbury Member of Parliament and great agricultural expert, shy and delightful, was seated beside his friendly and outgoing wife. We shared a small, family farm with them. Their tall sons (one named Douglas), much older than ourselves, whom we were awed by, went on soon to National Service, university and the world of work and therefore filled up the family pew on an irregular basis. They were a Wiltshire farming and political family; we were the same from Hampshire, although my father's own constituency was in Surrey. (Other nearby politicians, such as the Wantage Member, Airey Neave, and John Boyd Carpenter were familiar figures too.) The Palmer family, of Reading biscuit fame, filled up another brace of pews.

The older village spinsters or widows sat together, in hats and gloves, near the back, as the supporting cast or chorus of an opera. My father and Anthony Hurd, the two church wardens, read the lessons with dignity and care.

'The Lord is my shepherd; I shall not want' gave the answer to the sufferings of Job and Jonah. St John's Gospel gave us the statement of creation to match and surpass that of Genesis: 'In the beginning was the Word, and the Word was with God, and the Word was God.' Certainly we lacked nothing as children, either spiritually or materially.

The church interior was especially bright for festivals. Normally nature was kept outside the lich-gate, as if the strength of woods and fields might turn the worshippers away from the Christian invaders back to the primeval forces of earth, water, air and fire. But the power of large numbers of worshippers was evidently enough to conquer paganism and for once untamed nature overwhelmed the normal primness of the establishment. Ivy climbed up the gas-mantled lightposts, exuberant arrangements by my artist mother (who was taught to paint by Beatrix Potter's illustrator) spilled out of the pulpit and every window-sill was crowded with holly and orange and white winter berries. The aisle steps always held so much foliage that Matins, with no congregation movement, was a safer service than Holy Communion. The font was the apogee of decoration, bursting with leaves and branches, flowers and pussy-willow or evergreen – June, Peter Hiscock's wife, traditionally taking that as her work. Everything smelled fresh from the woods and gardens after the decorators had finished on festival days.

Bursting into song from a squashed position in front of the sopranos, we children looked across the two-foot aisle at the open-mouthed men – grand in their red robes, clean white collars below shining faces – fresh home from milking the cows or feeding the sheep and cattle, cart-horses or hunters, pigs, ducks and chickens. The vicar was tame in comparison. The choir and organist combined pagan fervour with godly worship to lead the congregation into the paths of righteousness by lifting the rafters with joy. We knew that miracles and happinesses came in all sorts of guises: watching the stream flow and stickleback fish dart under the wooden bridge on the way to school; while playing in the woods and fields; in feeding the pigs and chickens, calves and horses; or gleaning the corn by hand after the harvester had passed; making a bonfire; or while learning a psalm by heart or a Shakespeare sonnet, when the words juxtaposed to give a glimpse of heaven. 'O Lord, how manifold are thy works: in wisdom hast thou made them all', I sang with honesty; 'the earth is full of thy riches'.

I rebelled early against going to church. But my mother cunningly thwarted my stated intention – after a particularly boring service (my first, or second, at perhaps the age of three) – of staying at home for good, by gaining a place for me in the choir when I was under five. I was wholly satisfied by being at the heart of the service for, as I had said to her in my rebellion, the only purpose of church was the music. My favourite psalm was number 104. 'Praise the Lord, O my soul', I sang; 'Oh Lord my God, thou art become exceeding glorious; thou art clothed with majesty and honour'. I could not see why it was a psalm marked out for Evensong since it went on: 'Thou deckest thyself with light as it were with a garment; and spreadest out the heavens like a curtain.' Surely this verse displayed the brightest of daylight, the continuing light of eternity. How different from the words of Simeon, which we sang in harmonious A minor, 'Lord, now lettest thou thy servant depart in peace'. That was for the shadow of evening and, although suitable for him, was not a request I could see myself making. I liked being alive. My psalm was one of praise, the proper stance for all of us, I thought.

Certainly it was the right one for me. The brightness of God's eternity on earth and heaven was mine to worship and to exude and touch and feel. Singing in the choir was just a way of expressing all that happiness and rich colour, texture and sound. The proffered path to God for us was Christianity. What, though, of those people who were not born into a Christian community? Surely God could not forget them? Did they have their pathways to Him, too, which I did not yet know about? Our Christian worship in song was the experience of a joy in God that I sought each day and often found. As the hymn put it: 'The sun that bids us rest is waking our brethren neath the western sky; and hour by hour fresh lips are making thy wondrous doings known on high.' I knew that I shared my joy in God with worshippers world-wide.

Our organist was a miracle-worker. She struggled with a spastic condition and a cleft palate, that hampered both her gait and her articulacy. She could not sing in the choir (forming words that could be understood to a rhythm was too difficult) and her walk was jerky and unco-ordinated as she moved up the aisle. But on the organ she could lead with her hands just able to pull out the stops and manage the keys as well and her feet attempted a sporadic bassline on the pedals.

When I took over from her sometimes, at the age of eight onwards, I discovered that the true owner of the organ was the verger, Mr Davis. He worked the hand-powered bellows that gave the organ life. He had the power to break the smooth flow of sound, to disrupt the singers, confuse the musically wandering, warbling vicar or torment the tone-deaf curate (who was often muddy from a learner bicycle tumble). He brought a *frisson* of horror to the body of the church. If he withheld his raw arm energy at the bottom of the pumping circle, the bellows collapsed. A wailing, terminal sound like pigs at slaughter (familiar to a country child) filled the air finally and fled. The organist's fingers still sought to continue the falling phrase, pressing the silenced keys; no wind stirred the reeds in the organ-pipes and all in church fell silent. He became my enemy.

Sitting on the organ stool, I found a sweet revenge. There was a small crack in the organ loft through which, by twisting carefully, the organist could sometimes catch a glimpse of him sitting, scowling by the bellows' pump handle. During the sermon he took the biblical message of not working on Sunday seriously, and went to sleep. Beside his ear as he leant against the stone, in slumber, projected the whistle pipe. The stop for this was beside the great manual, and owned by the organist. Although it meant a subsequent economy with the truth – when explaining the interruption of his sermon to the vicar – I found that the satisfactorily sharp and harsh sound caused by pulling the whistle stop always penetrated the verger's ear-drum and woke him up. He hated it. The pulpit was only close enough for the vicar to hear a loud squeak, as the noise was well muffled by the old, thick, blue velvet curtain the verger drew to shield his sleep. The congregation heard nothing of the battle.

Besides, I had the backing of the choir, who were constantly aggravated by the verger: the four senior choirmen rang the bells to call in the congregation, a job the verger wanted; he cleaned the vestry where the choristers robed and it was said that he left the mouse-droppings there on purpose; he did not pay proper reverence to the large piles of music stacked up so carefully by the organist when he swept the choir-stalls; the list was endless and the feud was carried on in the pub and fields during the week's work. It rather negated the Bible's view that we should 'turn the other cheek'. Which view was right? It seemed that morally impeccable actions were not the ones that won. Or should we adopt a longer perspective, as in the story of the tortoise and the hare? Or was winning not the goal in any case?

I found the same kaleidoscope of experiences in faith, in action at my senior school, St Mary's, Wantage. Founded by the Anglican Community of St Mary the Virgin in the 1860s, the Order was the first Anglican nunnery since the reformation of Henry VIII. The nuns, an academic and spiritual élite, kept the full canon of the Church services, praying nine times daily as well as teaching. Their dedication to sustaining the recognition of and honour due to individual suffering anywhere was total. I watched and silently thanked them in my prayers and work. No question of faith was too large for them to tackle and I tried many challenges. Their extraordinary optimism allowed for jokes and teasing against each other and their pupils. Here again my cup of love, security and physical blessing was overflowing.

Comparative religious studies were brought alive for me by studying texts in the originals from time to time. My music teacher, Sister Sheila, was the convent's Hebrew specialist (she also led on plainsong). The Sister Superior knew Aramaic and helped me learn a little. Latin and Greek were curriculum choices. I chose them both. I also taught myself a scrap of Anglo-Saxon, to study *Beowulf*, and read the *Epic of Gilgamesh* out of Sumeria's civilisation. At home I had read the Koran from cover to cover.

Chapel, with organist and head-of-choir responsibilities, brought all my philosophical and religious explorations together in music. Voluntaries on the organ, hymns, psalms, chorales and cantatas in the choir; the world seemed permanently in song. For myself I knew that 'I will sing unto the Lord as long as I live: I will praise my God while I have my being' was a true statement. The plainsong Gregorian chants heightened the words' strength of purpose through tonal simplicity, without harmony or structure intervening. My organ teacher,

William Avery, was completely blind (a Second-World-War injury suffered as a soldier in his early twenties). His face and bearing beamed out joy in God as his manual and pedal power pushed Bach to ring in the rafters.

It seemed natural on entering the Royal Academy of Music that the first words we students saw on arrival were 'sing unto God'. They were emblazoned on the floor of the entrance hall in Gothic-revival scripted tiles. Each day I walked over them and sang in response in my heart.

My singing tutor, Henry Cummings, had sung with the great Kathleen Ferrier. His weakness was cigarettes, unheard of in a singer. And indeed he barely smoked the cigarettes; he lit them sequentially and, forgetful of stubbing out, was wreathed in smoke from different half-burnt cigarettes discarded in ashtrays in corners of his room. He claimed that it did not harm his vocal chords as he never inhaled. His fellow professors disapproved strongly and banished him to the top of the building. His preference was for German lieder; mine was for Bach chorales. *Wachet auf* in good, Germanic D major was rich in harmony, needed linguistic effort and was satisfactory translated on to the organ. We identified a mutual love of Richard Strauss, whose structured harmonies underpinned soaring romantic lyricism.

I found an outlet for my church music expression in the star-burst of services in London. Churches, chapels, cathedrals; all were there and open, with services of differing kinds and musical quality. The head of the Royal Academy, Sir Thomas Armstrong, begged me to spend less time singing in church and more in the Academy choir. This was a body we all despised as it included non-choral students. How could a flautist or a cellist be expected to sing to our standards? In their turn, they looked down on the lack of innate musicianship displayed by the topmost singers, who had heavenly voices but were not able to keep time, a primary musical requirement.

Sir Thomas Armstrong taught personal morality in an

unusual way. A student left before her exams due to an unexpected pregnancy. 'Girls, girls,' said Sir Thomas, 'never become pregnant; look how it interrupts your musical careers.' My mother's moral strictures were even more binding.

I joined the Bach Choir and sang in it, with sisters Rose and Laura and with musical cousins and friends, for several years. Filling the Royal Albert Hall with the *St Matthew Passion* or the *Christmas Oratorio* embedded the words and music in worship in secular surroundings. My Devon constituency, with green fields and woods studded with churches and chapels, gives those who live or visit there the same opportunities to worship in song and prayer that I had through my childhood and youth.

Coming into the House of Commons was a dive back into childhood. Whatever people may say, the structure and form of national politics in the United Kingdom is rooted and grounded in a belief in God, expressed in our establishment through the rites of worship of the Church of England. Some will think it hypocritical, but each day in the Houses of Parliament we start our work with private prayer. Away from public gaze and even apart from the servants of the House (clerks, badged messengers, police) but with our guard of honour, the Sergeant at Arms, who protects both Members and the Mace, the Speaker's Chaplain leads us in prayers that echo through centuries of democratic rule. 'Prevent O Lord and follow us', we assent to in unison 'Amen'.

Outside the Chamber, Members and the House staff have different patterns of private worship. The Speaker's Prayer Breakfast Group meets in the most elegant surroundings. A shortened 1662 Holy Communion is held regularly in St Margaret's, Westminster. Madam Speaker's official bedroom, with a vast, high bed and walls draped in red and gold brocade next-door to a humble, modern kitchen is laid up for toast, tea and coffee

afterwards. An official guest is given all of five minutes
for their spiritual message.

Once a year that group hosts the National Prayer
Breakfast, where British and overseas guest worshippers
meet for a breakfast of meditation opposite Westminster
Abbey in the new Queen Elizabeth Conference Centre.
Croissants, coffee and scrambled eggs are interspersed
with readings, music and prayer and followed by weighty
seminars all morning and afternoon. In 1992, the south-
west choirboy for two years, Darryn Watkin, robed up in
scarlet and white and bemedalled with choral tributes,
led the songs of praise. I accompanied him on a scratchy
upright piano.

Each Monday when the House is sitting, a study group
of Anglican Members meet for prayer just after lunch,
led by an external layman (a friend of all). Bibles are
given out and key passages read, with personal analysis.
As with the Speaker's Prayer Group, time is short; after
2.25 p.m. the room is empty of Members, now running
upstairs for official prayers, with a cluster of open Bibles
and notes left behind for tidying and removal by others.

Meanwhile, down in the chapel of St Mary's Underhill,
regular services are held for different denominations of
Christianity. The chapel is tucked away deep beneath the
great Westminster Hall. The huge timber hammerbeam
roof, eight centuries old, arches high over brass tablets in
the flagstones which mark past national triumphs or som-
bre historical moments. We pass over the declarations of
political impeachment, kingly execution and lyings in
state to burrow downstairs and reach the light and
gilded warmth of worship in chapel. Our concentration on
worship is only disrupted by the disharmony and creaks
of a very old organ.

Over the road (a hazardous crossing), St Margaret's,
our Commons Parish Church since the seventeenth century, floats in pale harmony of stone, a small barge
moored beside the anchored enormity of Westminster
Abbey. Trussed and pinioned, pinnacled and arched to

the ceiling of eternity, the Abbey is for the common people. We who represent them (not the House of Lords, whose grandees represent themselves) have our own humbler and friendly abode for worship. St Margaret's bells ring loudly for our carol service every December; packed and triumphant. In 1990 we had our own House of Commons *Songs of Praise* on television. On the other side of Parliament Square stands the four-square tribute to John Wesley's energy and vision. Eight minutes' walk down Victoria Street (the time taken up by the progress of a Commons vote) rests the intricate Roman Catholic cathedral.

All this worship, and more, for 651 Members of Parliament, and for the Lords and the staff of both Houses, too. Outside formal religious establishments (monasteries, convents and schools) is there any other group of people to whom so much Christian thought, support and leadership is offered? And is the effort of all these people, who give their time, their Christian witness and their shared religious confidences, reflected in a wiser, kindlier House of Commons?

Not everyone attends Church each Sunday, nor even on holy days, but surely the key to the need for worship in the Chamber is the weight of the power we hold as democratically elected Members. For, in our system, the House of Commons is omnipotent and omnicompetent. The vote is final and measures passed by the Commons only await Royal Assent (now a formality) before becoming law. Such power may be too large for people to handle untouched by God; for power corrupts, and incorruptibility is only found in God. Left to ourselves, our inborn self-protection can turn to selfishness, our natural energies can be channelled into personal ambition. Our unfettered love for others is even tainted and soured into hatred for those unloving in return.

The over-arching Christian value, the superordinate goal, is surely love of others. Jesus gave to his disciples and through them to us what He described as 'a new commandment': 'that you love one another as I have loved you'. Within the parliamentary system of the United Kingdom, love seems to be the most elusive value of all, and yet it is the one without which all our other personal values vanish.

The purveyor of God's love in the House of Commons is the Speaker's Chaplain, Canon Donald Gray. He is our parish priest, and friend of all. He is just there, thoughtful and with a cheerful eye alert to a signal of distress or just a need to talk from a member of his spiritual flock. Without him, I believe our individual efforts to find God would get short shrift, for the Devil can certainly find work for idling parliamentary hands and minds to do. He offers us God's peace within the political marketplace.

Sometimes we lift up our eyes from the floor of the House unto the hills, where far, far away we see very different hells on earth. There, evil has triumphed, apparently unchecked. Torture (in thirty-two new varieties), imprisonments underground for years on end, mass executions with families brought close in to watch just feet away. Dante's *Inferno* has been created on God's earth, in many, many places. Our stated European Christian heritage seems to have little effect.

Iraq or Bosnia, Somalia or Cambodia, the cries of those victims make our parliamentary conflicts fade from shouts to murmurs. Only when listening intently to the voices of the voiceless, and speaking for victims who cannot speak for themselves, do parliamentarians fulfil their proper role.

2

Images of Pain

From my earliest days, I felt both the joy of knowing God, and the injustice of human lives. Both were around me to see and ponder on. I was brought up on a farm, near the village of Winterbourne. Mental handicap was shown in the village by Jimmy the idiot. His mother, unmarried and unsupported, brought him up in a lonely existence. The village children threw stones at him and shouted as he shambled by, a meaningless smile on his face. He was taller and older than them, a young man and yet a child. I worried dreadfully for him, but saw no way of intervening.

My best friend of all times in my childhood was in the choir. Fred Glass, choirman boy and man, opened his mouth wide and sang to the vaulted roof with wonderful enthusiasm. He beamed with happiness and had a quieter brother. Bert Herbert completed the trio of firm supporters of the church; and there were eight or nine other choirmen.

The homes of many agricultural workers had outdoor privies at the bottom of short gardens. Many women's hands were really worn by washing and cleaning with harsh soap. I went with my father further behind the prim curtains of respectability. He visited his constituency every Saturday and there was always room in his car for a daughter or two. Indeed, he welcomed company. My mother rarely came, as with a husband, father, two

brothers and two brothers-in-law – and subsequently a
son-in-law and daughter – in Parliament, she saw politics
as a self-satisfying and anti-family activity and stayed
at home with poetry, water-colours and her gardening.
Her own form of community service was to work voluntarily for the local National Society for Prevention of
Cruelty to Children, and as National Vice-Chairman for
Dr Barnardos.

Perhaps I was about four years old when I had a
stark experience that has always lived in my memory.
Alone with my father, I visited a children's home, in
Farnham, Surrey, the heart of his constituency. It was
a large Victorian house with a vast garden, run by an
old-fashioned, strict and well-meaning matron. She had a
big, warm heart, but the possibilities open to her for doing
more than keeping her charges clean and cared for, were
very limited. I saw a child beside me, whose head seemed
oddly large. She was my height, her back was turned to
me. Then she turned round and I saw, with agony, that
this was a grown-up woman. She walked with enormous
difficulty, her limbs no larger than my own, her head was
gross, her spine was crooked. I reached out to her to make
friends, but age was against me and she turned away.

I could but marvel that her plight, so different from
my own, was unalterable, unfair, and that I equally had
no claim upon my physical ability, my mental agility,
nor yet my comfortable and happy home, by my own
right. It had been given to me. She had been given
something horribly different. My determination to make
a fairer world for others was born that moment. I saw
the gulf, unbreachable between us in terms of physical
ability, and knowing that I could not help her personally
then and there, I saw the future when I would be
grown-up and could find fairness. She was imprisoned
and I was free; she could not move fast and I could run;
she had no family and I had everything at home; she had
no place to go and I had the house and garden, the woods,
the commons and everything beyond. There was no blame

attached to either of us for our situation; it was the reality that we had been given. But as the one who was free, the one who could talk and laugh, the one who could have the safe background of family and home, I could run for her, I could speak in her name, I could change things for people like her and keep her in my heart. I knew that I could never forget her, nor the good-heartedness and relative powerlessness of the matron running the home. She was doing her best, although her best did so little to breach the gap between the child and the outside world.

Thinking about it afterwards, I concluded that the political forum was the place in which national change to help the ordinary person in difficulty could be made. Of course I knew that physical disability did not fall under political command. But there were other problems on which I saw my father working: listening to war victims, old ladies in great poverty, sick people without sufficient incomes to pay the bills, families without housing and many more. I saw that Parliament, if MPs were wise and thoughtful, could create ways whereby the needy could take authority for their lives themselves without unalterable, repressive social constraints. I joined my internal vow to help the helpless with one to seek to enter Parliament, to pursue change from within the establishment system that I honoured.

On the reverse side, it was clear that the House of Commons was a place nearly barred to women. They were there on sufferance. The system was a firmly masculine one and run by men. They only allowed in women sparsely and for the sake of form. I gained hope that I might be one of those few women when Dame Florence Horsbrugh, the first Conservative female Cabinet Minister, came to the constituency to make a speech and stayed the night with us. She had managed it and I would try.

An evil backdrop to my childhood was the Holocaust. Born in the Second World War, as I grew up the terrible fact emerged that millions of people had been deliberately destroyed because of the way in which they chose to

worship God. At first the knowledge was a dark cloud
'no bigger than a man's hand' on the horizon. Swiftly it
grew larger and darker until it seized the light entirely
and blacked out thought. The concentration camps had
been discovered.

No one ever explained to me why the Holocaust had
been allowed to happen. The only reasons offered on
behalf of responsible people with access to the appropriate
information was that 'they did not know'.

Of course there have always been times historically
when evil triumphed and even the bravest could not
win through. But to condone by pretending ignorance
of something that could never be hidden – the planned
destruction of 6 million people, executed in several countries and over a period of time – was to collaborate. We
had no right to cover up others' sufferings. Our obligation
was clear; we had to be the voice of the voiceless.

My first boarding school, which I started when I was
seven years old, reinforced my views on disability. There
was such a pretty child in my class, fair-haired and
blue-eyed, with the sweetest face. She was a polio victim,
though, and one of her legs was useless. At my second
boarding school a close friend from India, glossy black
haired and dark-eyed, Nazreen, had the very same horror.
Both were my friends and I loved them dearly. Nazreen
came from Poona and my other friend from Sussex. They
were a world apart, but in my mind they shone together
because of their approach to their difficulty. Each of them
ignored the useless leg they dragged behind them. Neither allowed it to impede their efforts and energies, except
in sport. I burned for them with the unfairness of their
beauty being disfigured, their energies being constrained
and their abilities to move around unhampered negated
by malfortune.

In another class there was temporarily a girl who
could not eat. She was all skin, eyes and bones and
seemed afraid of everyone. Teachers bullied her to try

to make her swallow. Children jeered at her miseries.
Mental disturbance seemed to me then to be even more
difficult to understand and help than physical disorder.

I had a physical constraint myself in sensory perception. My eyes and ears were always a problem. From birth
my ears were 'unsatisfactory for normal use' (a BUPA
comment when I joined the Save The Children Fund),
although I did not discover that they were a problem
until I was sixteen years old.

Eyes, however, were a different thing entirely. My sight
deterioration was discovered when I changed schools. I
took the eleven-plus at the age of ten and passed with
flying colours to enter St Mary's School, Wantage, run
by the Anglican Community of St Mary the Virgin. The
first thing the nuns did was give the new girls a medical.
An elderly doctor came along and I recall him putting
this chart upon the board in the gym and being unable
to read any letters on it. I was immediately whisked off
to the optician in Wantage and a pair of NHS glasses
were clapped on my nose. They were round and thick. I
could suddenly see clearly once again. I was so pleased.

My mother was appalled. The next thing I knew was
that I was rushed to London in the holidays and taken
to see an international specialist for eyes. Mr Benjamin
Ryecroft was a world-renowned figure. Right up at the top
of Harley Street he had a waiting room on the uppermost
floor. People with immense sight problems were queuing
up in front of me. Although this was his private clinic (he
was the leading surgeon at Moorfields Eye Hospital) he
saw cases of need, free and without restraint. I remember
sitting there, with men and women who could barely see
anything at all, awaiting his wisdom and consultation.

The real excitement for a child of ten was that he was
also the eye doctor for London Zoo. He told wonderful
tales, as he was inspecting my eyes on that very first
visit, of the treatment he had just given to an elderly
giraffe. He described with large amusement how the
giraffe's keepers had had such difficulty in getting its

head down low enough for him to see into the eye that in the end they had to make the animal unconscious.

Alas, even Homer nods and Mr Ryecroft (later Sir Benjamin) was no exception to that infallible rule. He was in the process of developing a theory that spectacles, or magnification through any means devised to help short sight, weakened the muscles of the eye. Spectacles, therefore, would have the effect of damaging sight as children grew. I turned into an experiment for this theory, which I heartily hope has been fully discredited. In a word, I went away from his consulting room that day without my glasses and with my sight a blur. It was a real disaster.

That, alas, was not the end of the prescription. My mother was instructed to ensure that I had an extra pint of milk each day and that I read for no more than an hour every day. My world fell in.

First, the extra milk at school. It was devastating. So much fuss was made about that wretched milk it was amazing that I did not turn into a hater of cows. The teachers through it was silly and that I had devised this burden to gain attention. They made full use of the nuisance value that I was causing them. Come break, come lunch, come tea there was the presentation of this wretched extra third of a pint that Emma Nicholson had to drink. It was always icy cold, straight from the fridge, and lay like a lump of ice on my complaining stomach. My classmates laughed, as every single day throughout the term I had to suck up the beastly milk from a miniaturised bottle. Added to which, it put me in the clutches of the school matron and that whole intrusive health world. She saw it as her duty (a kindly woman) to make sure that I drank it all up. So I was chased consistently by her, the junior matrons and anyone else she had to hand to make sure that I drank my milk. I felt a fool, particularly so when all this added richness put weight upon me speedily and for good.

The reading restrictions, however, were worse. Life had been my reading, probably because, although I did not realise it, my ears gave me too much difficulty for normal communication to be easy. I lived much of my world through books and managed very successfully, coming top of the class nearly all the time in my first two schools. To be divorced from reading was, for me, to be divorced from life. And it was very much more difficult for adults to enforce. What child can go through first, second and third form in their second school only on one hour's reading a day? So I was pushed out of class after class after class and who knew what to do with me?

Imagine my personal despair. I was sent for walks in the garden, more and more walks, and walks again until I knew every blade of grass and every tree and every sprouting shrub. I walked in and out of Chapel, up and down the corridors, all around the dormitories; anything to take away the weary hours until the class left the schoolroom and we had some meal or other breaktime. It was an impossible and intolerable situation. Of course I could not do my prep; how could I keep up? I was allowed neither to be in class nor to work on my books. It even hit my music since an hour's reading was deemed to encompass an hour's looking at music as well, so that I was unable to practise or to have proper music lessons any more.

Naturally, through desperation, I tried to get at books whenever I could. Equally, the teachers spent their time stopping me. The situation emerged whereby I, normally an easy person to teach, became an impossible pupil. When I was caught reading over the prescribed hour I was told that it would harm my eyes. I therefore lay awake at night wondering if in fact I was going blind and no one was telling me so not to upset me. Clearly it had to be that or why should the dictum be so inexorable and fierce?

Come holidays, the situation and private agony were almost worse. I had, throughout my childhood, spent hour upon hour upon hour reading through my father's large and varied library. I read the Koran when I was

eight, I was reading Trollope when I was eleven and
Jane Austen when I was nine and ten. *Hansards* were
everywhere throughout the house so it was possible to
get straight into politics. Latin, Greek and French novels
and history books were on all the shelves. It was the
richest feast that anyone could desire for reading. I was
curtailed from all of it and sentenced to a measly hour a
day. Walking in the garden, riding the pony, talking to the
dogs, talking to everyone I could find in my wanderings,
were occupations that were wholly insubstantial for me
in comparison to the world that lay within the covers of
those inaccessible books.

My school progress faltered and never really recovered,
although I managed A levels and grade VIII at piano
with distinction in performing and in theory. Home life
became a source of despair to me. With no other solace I
turned in on myself and stopped talking to my family or
to outsiders. Quite apart from anything else, discussion
was difficult since without realising it the deficiencies in
my ears had made me depend very much upon my eyes.
When my hearing disability was discovered it was said
at once by the specialist that I was a natural lipreader.
But without the ability to see (the world was a real fog)
I was cut off from that as well. I felt as if the world
was made up of 'reading police', with everyone tasked
to watch me and stop me following the only outlet for
my questioning mind.

I read guiltily, under the bedclothes with a torch at
night and diving away when footsteps came up the stairs
to discover that I was reading and take the book away. I
locked myself into the bathroom and used to hide books
under the bath. I took books into the stable and hid them
under the hay and straw. I put books into my satchel
and went riding on my pony for hours, tethering her at
a quiet and invisible spot and reading without anyone
there to see. I took books up trees at the far end of the
wood and read in the branches; I took books on long
walks into the village church and hid them under the

choir stools. Sir Benjamin Ryecroft presented me with a problem that I was unable to overcome because, as a child, I had no real control over my own actions. The grown-ups were all-powerful and I could only win against them by deceiving, something that was abhorrent to my nature and yet in which I partially succeeded.

Music had formed a large part of my life from the very beginning. At one time we possessed three grand pianos and an upright, too. One sister, Rose, played the violin, while my sister Laura, who went on to study at the Royal College of Music, and I, both took up the cello. All of us sang, and Harriet had a feel for rhythm in jazz. My mother, who played nothing and had very acute hearing, stayed at the far end of the garden – painting water-colour miniatures of flowers, perhaps on eggs for Easter – to escape our musical energy. Her deep embarrassment peaked in church or public places when we each took a different part of a hymn or song. For instance, I would sing the bass part, embellished floridly and sung two octaves up, reaching above top C. It was a genuine deterrent to her prayerful concentration.

Despite my music, ears were the other problem, but one that did not get discovered, as such, until I was sixteen. It happened like this. My mother's sitting-room was next-door to the dining-room. Both were modest rooms and were the original dwelling of the twelfth-century farmhouse on which our house was built. The wall between the two rooms was thick, four feet or more (the farmhouse had been two up and two down and the other rooms had spread around it later on). I walked away from my mother's sitting-room, leaving her in her armchair by the fire, and went through the door into the dining-room. My sister Laura came with me – three years older than myself, she had at that time just passed into the Royal College of Music. She said something over her shoulder to my mother as we stood just inside the door of the dining-room.

Suddenly Laura pulled me back into the sitting-room

and my mother was saying, 'I wonder if Emma is deaf? Perhaps that is the answer to the problems we have with her?' 'What do you mean?' someone asked. 'Well,' said my mother, 'I called through to both of them and only Laura responded. Let's try again and see if Emma hears what Laura hears when they are both the other side of that wall.' We went through again. I listened for her and heard no sound. Laura, with sharp ears, responded to an unseen call. We went back into the sitting-room. 'That's it,' said my mother, 'Emma must have something wrong with her ears. We must look into this.'

Some weeks later I was in a large and bright consulting room in Oxford with an elderly eminence on ears. He said he thought it unlikely that a girl of sixteen would be partly deaf and that no one would have noticed. None the less, he would of course test me. He wired me up with earphones fastened into a large machine that was in front of him. He did not make me turn my back and the result was that I watched his fingers fiddle. The game was to tell him when I heard a sound. It was extremely difficult to say that I had not heard a sound when I had seen his fingers creating one. However, I did my best and did not respond without hearing as I saw his hand move too often. I think the end result was not strictly correct and my ears were in fact worse than he put on his chart.

When he had finished the fifty-minute test he turned to my mother and told her that I had a considerable hearing loss. My mother, who had come in cheerfully expecting something very minor, if anything at all, looked appalled. I felt upset for her and reassured her quickly that I was sure it was a small problem and, even if it were large, what did it matter? The specialist added that there was no hearing aid available that could correct my hearing. I mentally shrugged my shoulders and decided to forget about it. My time on the return drive home was spent reassuring my mother, who was indeed upset. The most likely cause was the severe measles she suffered when five months pregnant with me. She wrongly felt guilt.

For me, however, although it was not referred to much more at home, the discovery came as a great relief and so many things fell into place: my great difficulty in being part of a group or enjoying a crowd, in having only a single close friend at any time actually became so much easier for me to understand. It did not of course help me in any way other than psychologically, since it did not improve my hearing. That only came much later on and coincided with my appointment as a Vice-Chairman of the Conservative Party in 1983. But at sixteen, having just started studying at the Royal Academy of Music, discovering this hearing problem meant I had to tell my professors about it. They were thoughtful and under-standing. We never discussed it again, although it might have been sensible in the musical context to have done so. I struggled very hard, very hard indeed, at the Royal Academy of Music to make sense of the sounds that I could not hear in order to give a good performance.

When I joined the Royal Academy of Music I took up voluntary work with disadvantaged young people in north London. This was a long-term effort run by a Mission Society out of Magdalene College, Oxford, established in the 1850s and still going strong. It was a sort of youth club, offering activities of a varied nature to the young people of a very poor district in London. I did my best to help, but not being a youth expert, worked better behind the coffee bar, washing up the mugs and making sandwiches. I did this on many evenings for a long while, with good intent, but could not see that my contribution made any difference to the youngsters' futures.

My admiration for those who did make a difference was large. An ex-policeman was the pick of the bunch, cheerful, buoyant, energetic and full of ideas. He corralled the activities and energies of a multifarious group of boys into constructive actions. I went with them all camping and undertook the cooking. Coping with the challenge of eighty youngsters in camps dotted round a huge Welsh field with few facilities was hard work for helpers. The

London children did not know the countryside and found it both lonely and liberating. Cooking for so many people on primitive stoves, fired by calor gas, in an enormous tent where everybody lined up, canteen-style, like junior soldiers, was a great experience. I learned from this voluntary work that the well-meaning intention 'good will to all men' is insufficient. Skills, experience and knowledge must be grafted on to achieve success.

I owe the correction of my hearing loss to two women older than myself. The Chairman of the Scottish Council of the Save The Children Fund, Nora King, introduced me to her hearing-aid dispenser in 1978. His aids, however, were not sophisticated enough to handle my complex hearing loss. Elspeth Howe, who also had a knowledge of this problem, noticed at a lunch with my sister Rose and MP brother-in-law Richard Luce – when they were entertaining herself and Geoffrey one Boxing Day – how left out of the conversation I had been. She offered the suggestion of John Goodwin in Marylebone High Street, London. He commented that he also thought there was nothing he could do because my hearing loss was so complex. But he gave me a challenge: he was prepared to try if I would work hard to help him. The trail to the basement in Marylebone High Street became familiar to me as I went back and forth while he tried out a huge variety of different instruments on me. It was a tough and difficult task and without the back-up of Sarah Keys, a bright and breezy Australian physiotherapist (the barrage of new and unfiltered sound caused a lot of pain), I might not have got through.

By the time I was appointed Vice-Chairman of the Conservative Party in May 1983 I could hear just as well as everyone else (and better than some). Added to which, a large amusement to me in the House of Commons, I still lip-read without thinking. It makes the mutterings of the Opposition Front Bench in Question Time clear to me immediately. I remember with irony the comments Neil Kinnock used to make to those sitting next-door to

him when one of Mrs Thatcher's most pungent comments
had pierced his political hide. I rarely let on that I knew
what he had said as that seemed rather unfair.

Hearing aids, and the glasses that I eventually acquired,
transformed my life. Suddenly I was locked into a different world where everybody appeared so bright and
keen and eager. The first impact of the possession of
my hearing aids came at a concert at the Royal Albert
Hall, in 1982, a day or so after I had acquired my first
pair for testing. I sat in heaven, listening to the richness
and balance of the instruments. Never before in my whole
career as a professional musician, practising and learning
from the age of three upwards, had I realised the exquisite
beauty and total harmony created by a full orchestra.
Tears of unique happiness ran down my cheeks. My
nice companion was appalled; he thought that I was
unhappy. When I explained it to him he still just could not
comprehend it. But who else could have done? Walking
in the garden, for the first time I heard the sound of the
birds! In the kitchen I heard the clatter of the pots and
pans behind my back. In the street I heard the slap of
shoes upon the pavement, and on the bus the rustle of
the clothes of the women sitting next to me. I even heard
the shuffle of paper as I turned the pages of a book. The
world was total, complete, all new and beautiful, as it
had been when as a child I first discovered the beauties
of the smells and colours of the flowers. I felt so thankful
to be alive.

I earlier experienced a little of the burden of physical
immobility, too. In 1969, on a holiday in France with
friends, I had fallen off a bicycle and cracked my skull
on a French country road. I recall little after that until
I awoke in hospital with vast and unending pain in my
head. After a week in hospital I struggled to get home.
The unwilling French doctors allowed me to do so (my
friends did not stop them) and my next memory was one
of physically collapsing in a large and noisy arena with
people walking past. It was Orly airport and a kindly

English businessman physically picked me up and with other helpers half-carried me on to the aeroplane. The cracked skull had indeed been serious and I remained in bed at home near Newbury in Berkshire for months, paralysed down my left side, both arm and leg, and unable to remember who I was, what my name meant or even how to speak. It took many months of pain to recover and it was curious to find that my body would not respond to the commands of my brain. My leg would not move, my arm would not move, words would not shape themselves and there was nothing I could do but stick it out. Again, it was my mother's worry that upset me more than anything else, more even than the enormous pain which would not dissipate. Little by little, movement came back, however, and syllable by syllable words re-emerged. A year later I started to play the piano and after eighteen months I was back at work. A new joy at being alive, with the physical capacity to absorb the beauties of the world again, helped with my full recovery. I never forgot that feeling, nor the experience of immobility.

My ears and eyes, before they were corrected, were a great irritant to me, a nuisance and aggravation. They held me up. However my growing concern for the disadvantaged did not come from these two problems. Perhaps because they were intrusive late in my childhood I never counted them as a handicap. They were not a determinant in my views on suffering. But pain was something different. The pain that I experienced from my head injury was constant and enormous. I vowed not to forget it, should it indeed go away. For I already knew that the body had this extraordinary programmed device to forget all pain. This is a wonderful thing, since if we recalled pain we could not advance at all. But I felt that it was of large importance for me to strive constantly to remember subsequently the pain that I had experienced. For I saw pain as the suffering that binds together those who have faced it and sets them fundamentally apart from other people. This is the real difference between us all. For pain shrinks your world to a burning needle of agony. It pushes out all other experience, all possibilities of learning, of gaining knowledge and communicating it, of seeing and sharing in the world's beauty.

Pain makes your world a narrow, deep shaft of torment and you are at the bottom. I felt that if I could recall on a permanent basis the pain I had felt so intensely, then I might understand a fraction of the problems others experience in their own pain. For unless you can do that you cannot enter into another's world of hurt, their narrow focus, nor understand their struggles to break past the barriers and continue living. And in a different way the small experience of part paralysis helped me in that task as well. The indignation of being unable to control my body was something that struck me forcibly. I did not mind for myself but it gave me an understanding of how an older person – whether in strange surroundings in a nursing home or hospital or somewhere much much worse such as a refugee camp – would be tormented by their inability to take care of themselves, to move around unaided, to link their mouth to their brain to be able to speak and say what they wanted to be heard. Those few months of part paralysis gave me a small glimpse of the problems of mobility and articulation that victims of strokes have to face, or that many older people experience just through the natural degeneration of their bodies.

Pain struck my mother too and I saw at close hand the effects of suffering on another person, someone whom I loved so much that I would truly have chosen to suffer in place of her myself. No sooner was I better from my head injury, and back in London working again in the field of computer software development (for McLintock, Mann and Whinney Murray in Southwark Street, London), than my mother fell ill for the second time with primary cancer in 1972. Surgeons said that this was a statistical impossibility, or nearly so, but she had it and doom stared ahead. I was enjoying being back in Southwark Street;

my colleagues had kept my job open during the time that my head had given me an unsought for space out of working life. It was fun and good to be back among those highly intelligent and amusing people, working on jobs as far-flung as the Middle East and southern Africa.

My mother's illness was traumatic. This time it was cancer of the brain. Whisked by a wonderful specialist into the hospital in Oxford she had an operation. He promised her, at her request before the operation, that he would tell her the whole truth. When she came round he told her that her time was limited indeed. Added to that huge grief came total paralysis (cancer of the brain does that to you). This was swiftly followed by total blindness. A little while later deafness followed too. My mother was extraordinary then as always. She decided to learn Braille and sent for all the books. She learnt big Braille, she learnt it fast and she began to teach herself to read. Before her hearing went entirely we joined the Royal National Institute For The Blind and we sent for all their book tapes. These proved singularly insufficient and much too slow to come. I therefore took up reading for her, hour upon hour upon hour reading through her favourite books. (I offered to record books for the RNIB but was not accepted.) I went home and put my job on hold again. One of my sisters was there too. My other two sisters came as often as they could and the four of us together nursed her at home over a fifteen-month period to her final end.

My father, who adored her, was distraught. After all, had she not promised him, at his request, each night as they went to sleep, that she would not die before him? He had believed her and did not think she would. He could not accept that she was dying and for a long time he forbade us to get any nurses in at all.

It was incredibly difficult. None of us was trained in nursing in any way, perhaps myself least of all with no husband or children to care for physically. It took months before we could persuade my father that even a modicum of nursing would be helpful. On top of that, because my mother was seen as a failure (after all she was dying) the medical profession took no further interest in her at all. I think the doctor came just once or twice during the whole period of time. The Church too stayed away; I just do not know why. Perhaps the vicar, a young and thoughtful man, felt shy of her. Either way he just did not come at all frequently and as my mother was a deeply spiritual woman, she missed that enormously.

Half-way through her illness she came with me to the Dorothy Kerin Nursing Home, a place founded by a wonderful Christian woman who was also a healer. Straight-down-the-line Christianity expressed through the provision of gentle comfort and care was what the nursing home offered. I happened to be one of the trustees at the time since the Southwark Street partnership for which I worked had been asked to carry out a small charitable consultancy task there to help them sort out their accounts and plan better for the future. As a result of that I became attached to them. (My godmother was a trustee too.) It was a wonderful setting and my mother spent a peaceful week there.

Throughout my mother's illness my father continued his post-Parliament work of helping the mentally handicapped and the psychiatrically ill. He became chairman of some hospitals dealing with the health of the mind at the request of the Labour Health Minister Richard Crossman and worked hard to improve conditions for staff and patients for ten years. The hospitals were very large. They had been built some miles outside towns so that sensitive residents would not be disturbed by mentally unsound people. Visitors were very, very few and the staff were superhuman.

Even the medical profession looked down on those qualified and caring for mental health patients. The training was a year less than for general medicine and this seemed to breed professional disdain. Dr O'Gorman, the chief psychiatrist of the largest hospital, had a good tale to tell – he left the hospital gates in his car, turned on to the main road and saw an upturned vehicle with the driver sitting on the verge looking confused. 'Can I help you?' he said. 'I'm a psychiatrist.' 'No,' came the immediate reply, 'I'm a gynaecologist and I'd rather wait for an ambulance.'

Dr O'Gorman was a specialist in autism and had a children's hospital-cum-home at Henley under his care. The children there were locked in silent self-communion. The staff gently coaxed and teased and taught. The children's reactions were negligible. Just occasionally there was a small breakthrough. One child made such progress that she very nearly went to ordinary primary school. She did not make it. The staff's personal investment in her and in the others seemed total.

Mental health care brought many amusements in its unpredictability. One senior doctor, named Dr Arkle, went to Newbury Races and saw an elderly lady who seemed oddly familiar. He wondered if she was a patient or a patient's mother. He wandered up and she was friendly (and in good health). She commented on the coincidence of names with Arkle, the famous race horse. She moved away and friends surrounded him, asking eagerly: 'What did the Queen Mother say?'

The mental health work went on as my mother got worse. Her illness was teaching me a great deal. Already I had discovered that the world was a world for the able-bodied. People's adverse reaction to mental health was common knowledge in our family, but their reaction to complete physical decay was new to us. The world seemed split into two halves, as with the reaction to mental patients: one half loved and laughed with the sick patient as if she were well again, the other 'walked by on the other side' as did the Levite in the parable of the Good Samaritan. Death later gave a sharper version of that human response.

My mother's tumour on the brain had by now caused total disability. This meant, as we discovered quickly, that public movement was nearly impossible. Even with the best of wheelchairs, getting on a train was frankly impossible. A bus was out of the question. And the car was difficult, with seats unmanoeuvrable to accommodate her needs. Pavements had barriers and obstructions, and the kerbstones were not flattened for wheelchair ease of movement. Entering shops was a major problem and many people seemed to react oddly to someone without mobility.

My mother's final horror set in in earnest. One day, when I was sitting by her bed, she opened her eyes and looked up at me, sightlessly. She asked that if the pain got too great to bear, would I give her a dose of pills, which would be all the bottle (morphine), and ensure that she died. I said that I would. A look of profound relief passed over her face and she went back to sleep. About a week later in October 1971, she died.

A greater personal understanding of suffering has given me a large admiration for others who are worse afflicted, putting up with pain for year after year after year. The small problems I have had myself have given me too a belief in the value of others. Friendship means so much; friendship is the best thing you can offer anyone in pain, anywhere. But most of all, I know now that we are in God's hands at all times. If you can see life as a pack of cards, realise that God deals the pack but asks you to play best in every way and at all times the cards given to you. You can't choose the pack, but you can indeed choose what you do with what is in your hand. Even in suffering you have that power, that individual choice and personal responsibility.

I was grateful to the experts for their knowledge but know too that they are bound by the known limits of discovery and excellence; they are not God. Mr Ryecroft, for example, did the very best he could with his new theory for my eyes. The fact that it was disastrous for me was not his fault; he used his knowledge to what he thought was my best advantage. That was his finest gift.

Surely the task of all of us is to give our best work to God, whatever that work may be and to do so irrelevant of our circumstances. For is that not the finest form of worship?

3

Political Systems, Personal Struggles

Sickness, despair and disability in our Western society are difficult to cope with and to ameliorate, but in the Third World they create a personal and permanent disaster. The developing world is too deficient of resources to have any surplus for the treatment and continuing care of the disabled. My first experience in Africa came when I was twenty-two. I had left the Royal Academy of Music six months before and took a leap laterally into a totally different field of work. Frustrated by my hearing handicap, which forced me to work musically through a wall of skewed sound, I passed my exams and decided to leave music alone for a while. To be a Licentiate at the Royal Academy of Music and an Associate at the Royal College of Music was reward enough for the moment. Maybe something would happen, I thought, that would bring me back to music later, but enough was enough, and struggling to break through a brick ceiling any longer was just folly. My sound capacity was against me. If I could not hear the flutes or violins, how could I expect to play a perfect piano concerto? I had to accept that it was just not possible.

But what should I do? I had to earn. I taught music as a temporary teacher but with no enthusiasm. My mother urged me to become a secretary and I refused. I temporarily became a cook, which was chaotic. I could not cook, and my first effort at roasting what turned out to be a frozen chicken (our own were fresh, which I could pluck and draw), as a Universal Aunt, was a fiasco; the raw and blood-dripping carcass was pushed back in silence through the hatch to me in the kitchen by the unfortunate dinner-party host and hostess. Although I cut it up into pieces at once with the breadknife and put it under the grill (a sporting initiative, I thought), I was not invited back. My second effort was even crazier. We had an Aga stove at home with flat-bottomed kettle. I was unclear as to how the oddly shaped kettle in my new employer's kitchen was designed to work. The oven and hob were gas, which after a struggle I mastered and lit. Twenty minutes later, I smelt an oddity and turned round to discover that the legs of the electric kettle had melted off under the heat of the gas flame. The only successful meal I cooked was for the ever warm-hearted Lord and Lady Whitelaw, who understandably invited me to do something which was really only warming up a dish she had already cooked. Even I could not fail with the washing-up.

I tried a City of London cooking job, taking it on the second day from a qualified Cordon Bleu cook, a friend of my sister Laura's. She offered it to me unofficially because the company accountant had made a mildly improper advance. She thought that I could fend him off and that no one would know the difference. I felt both points unlikely, but rose to the challenge. They spotted by Friday that I was a different cook to Monday's child. But they retained me for a while until, exuberant with their money in purchasing cooked food, I gave them five expensive and rich courses each day with different wines and they did no work. The partnership, the oldest stockbroking firm in the City, went bankrupt. Later, I cooked in Eire, but 200 hot-air balloonists from a dozen countries caught Salmonella (more frozen chickens) and were grounded because of me. Several competition days were lost. Professional cooking was not for me. In any case, I found the job satisfaction insubstantial as the results of my work were eaten up.

Those brief efforts brought me a few pounds, which was help for the indigent daughter of a Member of Parliament (my father's salary was £600 a year from the House of Commons), but my search for a career was under way. I wanted a real challenge, and one that used my brain and my concern for others to full extent.

I therefore turned to family connections and asked my father to introduce me to Conservative Central Office. But there I had no luck at all; they could not see any way in which I could be of use to them. I asked timidly about a junior research appointment, or about just making the tea. The answer was no, there was nothing that I had to offer them. Neither music, nor history, nor a strong desire for social change, nor a Conservative commitment appealed to the Smith Square hierarchy. My services and skills were just not wanted there. Somehow my years of constituency effort for my father (canvassing, helping at meetings, fêtes and Branch events, even the occasional little speech) did not weigh in my balance either.

I found my challenge in the world of computer software development – then a new and fascinating industry, still young enough to be largely experimental. I heard the word 'computer' from a friend. I didn't know what it meant, nor what computers did. But it sounded exciting and I vowed to try to get into that new world.

Some weeks later, and after a large struggle ('The last thing we want is a non-working musician,' said the Personnel Director sharply), I found myself sitting the entrance exam for International Computers. This vast British company, now ICL, had a wonderful training programme. Low pay meant that those trained slowly and well, swiftly left. But they had a well-honed entrance exam and I was allowed to sit it as an experiment. The day was long and hot and I sat in a vast room on the sixth floor of their Putney head office, with the sun pouring in on sweating graduates of maths and sciences. I was as happy as a lark. I knew I had no right to be there and wasn't going to get any further. I just enjoyed my day, with paper after paper pouring on to my desk for answers. It was indeed fun, and I set my wits to work. I had nothing to lose and it was a lucky and exciting experience. At the end of the day, the one jarring note was introduced: they took away my rough paper, which was a slight embarrassment – I could not multiply, as my school had allowed me to opt out of maths at eight and I therefore added thirty up fifteen times on paper. Then we had a brief interview (a ten-minute talk) and that was it. To my astonishment and eternal happiness, a week later I got a letter inviting me to join them.

The training course meant living-in at Cookham Deane for several months. After an hour of the first lecture, I realised my only hope was to ask questions on everything I did not understand, and that was just about the whole of the first hour's discourse. I put my hand up and was called. What was the difference between positive and negative? I asked. The wrath of Zeus descended and I was fortunate to outlive the blast. My fellow students were astounded to find a cuckoo in their nest. They crowded round me at coffee-break asking if I had really meant it. On discovering that I did, they settled down and morning, noon and night they taught me basic maths. The publican gave me milk as I could not stomach the nightly beer ritual. About a week later, something clicked in my head. I watched a tutor charting a program pattern on the board and realised that she and the students were trying to write a fugue, but in a different language and that they didn't know how to do it. Swiftly I turned my thinking upside down and addressed the problem musically. In my mind's eye I swapped all my musical terminology for their words (which I was learning fast) and mentally I wrote the work in fugal mode with mathematical terms. Within a year, I was the teacher, and writing the teaching manuals, too.

ICL was an early good employer. In my first year's

class I taught a quadriplegic (a polio victim), and someone without his sight. I also had as a pupil a torture victim out of Romania (fifteen years spent in a cell crammed to the ceiling with bunks and people), and someone from Poland whose family had been killed in Auschwitz. These two were students who were over the normal recruiting age whom ICL had taken on to see if mature people could learn this extraordinary new profession. The two handi-capped men were there because ICL was an employer of large heart and breadth of thinking. It was a wonderful class and we achieved outstanding results. ICL then used us as a test bed for shortened entry exams.

At the end of my four-month teaching session, I was called up to the sixth floor again to see the boss. He told me to go to Africa the following day. 'Why me?' I asked. I knew my relative lowliness in the ICL scale of things. 'Because you are the only one who looks even half-way respectable,' he replied. I looked down at my Marks & Spencer tartan skirt and dark-green twin-set and thought of my far cleverer colleagues with their firsts in maths and sciences, clothed in scruff order. What did appearance have to do with ability? Surely it was a *non sequitur* – did he need to learn logic? Maybe I should teach him the science of Euler's Circles or Venn's Rings that I was studying in my spare time.

'What shall I do there?' I asked.

'Do nothing, there's nothing that you can do. We have sold the Government of Northern Rhodesia a computer that will not work. But they have only paid half the bill and we want them to pay the other half. In the meantime, the Finance Secretary, a senior Colonial Office civil servant, has come over to complain to the Government of the United Kingdom. I had the Foreign Office on the telephone this morning and they want us to put it right. They have said that the Government of Northern Rhodesia will not pay the other half of our bill until we have done so.

'However,' he went on, 'it's beyond you to put the

computer right (you're not a hardware engineer), but I can't find a hardware engineer to go out there and do the work. You, therefore, are to go there now as they are demanding immediate action and to sit there, doing nothing, but appearing as if you are carrying out some work. This will keep them calm and maybe they will pay the bill while I try to find an engineer to make the machine effective.'

I thought that rather a raw deal to offer to the Government of Northern Rhodesia and tried to say so but was overruled. The following day, after a few swift injections and carrying two cotton dresses in a plastic bag, I found myself on the aeroplane going to Africa for the first time. Looking down as we flew over the Sahara desert I wondered how I could possibly sustain an image of action when I was doing nothing. I could not combine the two conflicting aspects of my brief.

I was proved right. On my arrival I was met with a panoply of people who had come to welcome the expert from the United Kingdom who would work Western magic. I stayed in the Ridgeway Hotel and every day I was picked up and taken to the Ministry of Finance, down the Commercial Road. There – through ranks of British and African clerks, each keeping wonderfully large ledgers filled with copperplate writing, or near copperplate – I went to the bowels of the Finance Department and found the errant computer. It was indeed a disaster. Soon after its installation, some three months earlier, it had broken down, not once, not twice, not even three times, but five times running. On the sixth attempt to get it going the International Computers' engineers had reported to the head of department that it was fully mended and could fully function. Would they please pay the bill? they asked. The Finance Minister himself, a tall and elegant African, newly appointed for the coming independence of the State of Zambia, had come downstairs. He had walked into the machine room and done something rather unusual. He had jumped up and down. With a crash, the entire false floor had broken, and half the cables had been ripped to bits. That was the last straw for the Government and the Finance Secretary had gone to the airport and flown to England on the very next flight. This was the man who met me at the airport and the following day I met the Minister. Both of them expected large and determining actions from me.

There was only one thing for me to do, and that was to try to fix the problem. The alternative, which was unacceptable, would have been to carry out the instruction given to me by my boss, that I was to do nothing. This would have displayed both ICL's professional incompetence and its shabby treatment of a British colony.

Reconciling those two irreconcilables could only be achieved if I found the answer. I stared at the machine and it offered no thoughts. I turned away and decided that I had to think differently. Maybe I could find a solution that was not hardware based? I asked if I could study the work of the Department and agreement was given immediately. The following day I took my notebook and sat beside the Senior Clerk. Within half an hour the full extent of the horror ahead for the upcoming State of Zambia displayed itself. The clerks, British in origin and highly trained, albeit lowly paid, were carrying out ledger work which would have been deemed excellent in Charles Dickens's City of London. Ledger upon ledger of accurate work was displayed in front of my gaze. I saw, however, that this work was the work that was keeping the State going: pension payments, salary payments, any Social Services work and the budgets for education; everything streamed through this Treasury of activity. I saw also that the Africans, fired up with excitement and enthusiasm for the independence of their beloved State, were in no mood to carry the work on. Nor did I think that they had been trained to understand the need for the work; somehow the Colonial Office had not seen in sufficient time that independence would be on the way and they were only now trying to pull in

the African contingent and train them in the senior
managerial techniques which would enable the work to
continue to flow.

I looked out of the window and saw some disabled
African pensioners shuffling past. I realised that their
pensions, meagre though they were, would stop once
these great ledgers were slammed shut for the last
time, fastened and stored away. They would not be
opened up the day after independence, of that I was
certain. Everything would slowly, or swiftly, grind to
a halt, and the State would face a really impossible task
in keeping the systems going. And yet I could see that
ICL, in its wisdom, or lack of it, had not planned for
these systems to be created and transferred on to the
electronic media. I could not understand how they had
sold a piece of hardware at vast cost to the Government
and had not worked out what on earth they were going
to do to fill it up with the essential tasks. This in itself
was a greater tragedy, since this was the new and
complex side of the business. Bits of equipment could
always be kicked into life by somebody really skilled and
experienced (I knew that from Putney), but system design
and software creation were arcane mysteries to most
people. Yet it was on that work that the administration
of the new State of Zambia would have to depend.

I settled down to work. I sorted out systems, drew
flow-charts, made copious instructions and then after
three weeks of intensive work I thought that I had
better call my boss. To my astonishment, the telephone
worked and I got through to the great man himself. I put
forward a proposal, outlined the problem and suggested
that I flew it back to Britain, that the work that I had
created was programmed there and that I put it on the
Southern Rhodesia computer for it to work and flew the
results up and down to Northern Rhodesia every week.
To my astonishment, he accepted and said my class had
just completed their final tasks after my departure and
all twelve of them would be ready waiting to work. He

would allocate another twelve people too. A full team of skilled, experienced and trained programmers would therefore be waiting for me at Heathrow.

With joy in my heart I went back to the Permanent Secretary and to the Minister and told them what I had done. I warned them that it would cost another large sum of money, but I explained that this would have happened in any case, it was merely that no one had explained this to them first. They had seen how hard I had been working (right into the evenings and at weekends too), they knew that I was on their side in wanting to make the State efficient and perform effectively subsequent to independence, and we were by then close friends. They therefore accepted the prospect of a further large payment (the hardware was still not put right, despite the continuing effort of a small engineer who had flown up from Salisbury, Southern Rhodesia) and I flew off back to London with all their blessings.

For some months subsequently, right up to a year later, I was still flying in and out of Zambia, bringing in pieces of work, establishing them, creating new work and taking it back to London. The Putney teams outperformed themselves and it was a magnificent success.

Six months after my initial visit, the Foreign Minister and myself took the floor as the only mixed-race couple for the Zambian Independence Ball. It was a very odd feeling; neither he nor I saw anything extraordinary about our celebrating together, but the whole room shrank away from us and I saw as we spun round alone that half the room was full of people with white skins and the other half was those with black. We took the decision together to go on dancing as a personal joint statement of racial colour-blindness. My heart sank at the continuing racial divisions of life in Africa despite independence.

I visited Malawi for the first time also in 1964 – the same year that I went to Zambia. That was a great excitement because I joined my father for Malawi independence. Dr Banda, the incoming President, had

invited one person from every Member of the United
Nations, but of course the United Kingdom, as the ruling
power handing over the reins, sent a larger delegation.
After the celebrations were over (a mixture of pomp and
ceremony amid large poverty) my father and I stayed on
as Dr Banda's guests in the palace and spent our time
for a few days seeing behind the scenes. We went into
the bush and saw an enormous leper colony with 750
men, cared for by the French White Fathers. The men
cried when we shook their arms (no hands were left) or
patted their shoulders. They were the complete outcasts.
I thought of Christ and the leper. How did He handle the
social horror His actions caused?

My father and I visited the hospital and saw the paucity
of provision. There was just one qualified doctor for the
whole of Malawi. I concluded again that governments
must take responsibility on behalf of society for assisting
the poorest of the poor. It was clear that society alone
would not. Surely the Colonial Office could have done
more. I realised that independence had caught many of
the Colonial Office civil servants unawares. We saw the
difficulties of the disabled struggling to live, ignored by
their families because there was nothing that could be
done to help them. It made a large impression on me since,
without my professional computer hat, I had nothing to
offer. We went on to Kenya and to Tanzania, and saw the
same situations replicated throughout that part of Africa.
My mind was thinking always, seeking ways of providing lasting assistance without the white support-system
that had brought order and some measure of prosperity
throughout the colonial years.

Back in London, I continued to work in the evenings as a volunteer in the youth-club mission. Without the real skills of youth training that my other
friends in the North London mission clearly had, however, I felt my contribution was inadequate. Certainly
some of us were performing a very useful task, but I
was uncertain as to whether I fitted into the puzzle.

ICL management concluded that I had the new systems analysis skill and sent me for a further five months living-in training course. Brandenham Manor, Disraeli's old home, was the backdrop for intensive and challenging learning with five others. I practised the organ at lunch-times in the estate church in the garden. An orthodox Jew worked the bellows using one hand on the pump (his left) and doing *The Daily Telegraph* crossword puzzle on his knee with his right hand. He gave me supper at Blooms, the famous Jewish East End London restaurant, at my request. My lack of familiarity with the menu led to a lady opposite asking my colleague if his mother knew that he was supping with a gentile. Religious divisions seemed very sharp and almost overwhelmed our professional partnership.

I started to explore the possibilities of becoming a probation officer. I also joined as a junior member of the Inner Temple, with the idea of reading law and becoming a barrister. But finances were against me for that one; I soon discovered that it was an expensive business and I was not eligible for a grant. All of these thoughts and explorations arose from the juxtaposition of my boredom within ICL (I was carrying out an internal study on cost accounting procedures, a drab exercise with no immediate benefit to anyone) and my continuing concerns for those in need in both overseas countries and also in Britain.

Running alongside my professional work, however, I had noticed a lot of problems encountered by the developing world countries. Firstly, the political problems. I saw the beginnings of such enthusiasm for democracy, generally with a socialist flavour, and the way in which somehow it narrowed the perspective and ended up in disaster. I saw the billions of pounds poured in by Western donors, the impracticability of some of the projects that they chose to finance, the distortion of need which their money brought, given the conditions that they attached to it. I saw, above all, the way in which little of the monies poured in ever enhanced the lives of those invisible people beneath the surface of society – the poor, the sick and the immediately unappealing.

In my heart of hearts I knew that political solutions were the most profound and ones that, if properly effected, lasted and gave the greatest benefits to others. All other work was palliative, covering up an unfair or inadequate situation. I concluded, therefore, that although I could not see the immediate impact of my professional work upon the poor and the unfortunate, that none the less continuing in the environment in which I flourished, computer software development and systems design, was best. I changed from one of Britain's largest companies to a small one and spent a happy and productive few years as one of the consultants for John Tyzack & Partners. I was their information technology expert. As part of a multi-disciplinary team dealing with blue-chip companies in difficulties, we worked hard and briskly. Colleagues were drawn from different professions. We produced first-class reports with thoughtful and productive recommendations which our clients up and down the United Kingdom and overseas adopted and which made them more profitable and more efficient.

Months spent in the East End of London with one client were a reminder of an older, slower world. The directors of that particular company arrived at 10.30 in the morning. The workers arrived at 7 a.m. and had their lunch-break in a very old canteen. The directors went out for lunch for a couple of hours to the nearest five-star pub and came back nearer 4 p.m. than 3 p.m., and left an hour later. The workers did not respect them. The company was going downhill fast.

We decided on a simple course of action, namely, to follow the starting hours of the workers and their lunch-break hour (it was forty minutes only), which we took with them, and to leave after the entire workforce and the directors had left. This meant a gruelling programme for us, rising at 5 a.m. to get to the far end of London and beyond in order to start at 7 a.m., before the gates opened for the workmen. A break for a brisk and simple lunch with hot, sweet tea and then we stayed until 7.30 p.m. at night. We worked solidly throughout the entirety of the twelve-hour day. It soon showed results. The directors were shamed into beginning earlier, the workmen respected us and we discussed the problems with them (they knew more about it than the directors did). In the end we turned the company round and it is now a flourishing concern once more.

In truth, I have always found that the highest business ethics match the highest ethics, or surpass them almost, of any religious group I have known. Good business demands high standards, and integrity in dealing with other people and with yourself. The virtues of hard work, consistency of attitude and scrupulous concern for the customer, the worker and the shareholder are the hallmarks of the best of British companies or any company world-wide. Business is an environment in which all the finest qualities of each religion can be brought out, in which the best of human behaviour patterns can be found and where excellence can flourish unhindered.

I compared my new standards in business, found in so many of my colleagues, with those self-same standards practised in a different way by the nuns at Wantage or by the farm workers in and around our village. Excellence can be everywhere and in every field of endeavour, if we but wish it to be there. Pretence is not enough; action must be real to justify human thought and optimism.

I returned to Malawi in 1985 to celebrate Kamuzu Day, the Presidential birthday. One-party corruption was deeply entrenched. Dr Banda was Life President without opposition. He was using the purity of the state against a racial group. The Indians were no longer allowed to keep village shops. They were forced to move to urban areas because they had been too successful. Only indigenous Malawians could now trade in the rural areas, where eighty per cent of the population still lived. Some of those Indian Malawi emigrated to Britain. One family opened a shop in London's East End selling Kosher food in competition with the local community traders. His shop was fire-bombed and his family attacked for their success in offering lower prices and attracting trade. I thought when I read of this in the London newspapers of the courteous compliment of my Malawi Foreign Ministry guide who, when I challenged her country's policy on racial prejudice said, 'Maybe we are not as civilised as Britain; we have a long way to go in learning racial tolerance.' How wrong she was.

In 1986, I visited Zambia again. This time it was to train volunteers and Government staff from twelve African countries in the skills of voluntary organisation on behalf of the Duke of Edinburgh's Award Scheme. It was a one-week course and their Overseas Director had asked me to participate for a forty-eight hour period, which I was glad to do. I heard a whisper while I was there that the Zambian Finance Department remained intact, still operating with work continuing to be flown up each week from Harare. I wondered what that could be, remembering my own systems efforts and organisation using that very route for work.

The head of Zambia's volunteer youth movement, the Director of the Boys Brigade, sought me out one evening. He told me of his lovely small daughter, Twiza, and her need for urgent heart surgery. I met with her and her family, and with the paediatrician, a Zambian trained in London. He said that only Great Ormond Street Children's Hospital could help. Nothing available in black Africa would be good enough professionally to meet her surgical needs.

In London, I took her case history to Great Ormond Street. The surgeons said that she had such a small chance of surviving open-heart surgery that they were unwilling to try. They could not cost it either, but upward of £250,000 would be needed. The parents, with whom I corresponded, begged for anything. I linked up with the best surgeon in South Africa, a white man. He took on

her case and she flew to Johannesburg. It was so right
to find a white surgeon in South Africa crossing the
apartheid line. We did our best (I paid myself, as in
the short timescale I could not find another donor) but
Great Ormond Street wisdom eventually proved correct.
Her parents renamed her and although she had some
more short years of life, little Emma-Twiza's grave is in
Lusaka.

After I had been elected to Parliament in 1987, I went
as House of Commons representative to Zambia, as a
member of the Commonwealth Observer team to monitor
the multi-party general election in October 1991, the first
for seventeen years. Here I found tragedy of a different
sort. The struggling country, led for over thirty years
by another form of dictator from Saddam Hussein, but
still a monopoly ruler, Kenneth Kaunda, had lost its
head-start, given by the copper mines' natural wealth,
through mismanagement and the world fall in prices.
Faced with difficulties, Kenneth Kaunda had returned
to one-party rule, as is the way in Africa. Weaving and
ducking, he had himself avoided the charge of corruption
that others had tried to pin on him by vesting the largesse
which he accrued upon his wife. In her name, for example,
was the house in Hampstead, valued at £3 million. The
dawn of promise that I had witnessed in 1964, when as
a young man he had taken up the reins of leadership
with such possibilities ahead, had long since gone. The
country was destitute economically, with the profits from
the copper mines foreclosed to South Africa for years
ahead.

It was an honour to be part of the Commonwealth
Observer team. Secretary General, Chief Emeka Anyaoku,
an old friend, had invited me to join the Commonwealth
Observer permanent team some time before. This was
my first opportunity to do the job. Jean Fryer, competent
and bustling, was our on-the-spot organiser. In Lusaka,
I met again the former Finance Minister, my elegant
friend, and he took me to his Department, where my

same computer systems were still functioning, intact with
the software that I had left them. I was astounded.

I and another team member, Mr Ahmed, of Bangladesh,
a former High Commissioner to London, were given the
task of monitoring Northern Province. We flew up to
Kasama, the major town, and met our driver Nelson
Muloonga in a serviceable Land-Rover-style vehicle and
were driven to the Kwatcha Relax Hotel, a real misnomer.
My room was in the basement, beside the kitchen, with
a small dusty window overlooking an open-sewage-ditch-
style waste-disposal yard. Large cockroaches, the size of
dinner plates, served instead of pictures on the walls,
except that they moved and scuttled away into the hanging cupboard immediately the door opened. The bed had
other creepy-crawlies in its over-used mattress, slender
as a board. We had been well briefed in Lusaka by the
experienced Commonwealth Secretariat team. Our task
was to monitor the elections, to identify and, if possible, to
correct imbalances of fairness and report back to Lusaka
after the ballot had been counted and declared within
our area so that the final report reflected faithfully
the democratic or non-democratic process in operation
throughout the country. In any case, Mr Ahmed knew
the system as he had been a Commonwealth Observer
before. He was an old hand at the business.

Our task was indeed a large one. The Northern Province of Zambia is half the size of England. It has only
one road, from south to north and, coming off that, a
multiplicity of wide, narrow and yet narrower red-earth
tracks. The term 'the bush' gives images of thick for-
estation. Zambia's Northern Province is a long horizon
of scrub, with tall trees and villages intervening. The
Zambezi River flows through, gathering strength on its
long journey south. Eventually it enters Zimbabwe at the
great Zambezi Falls. Not only roads but also transport
was scarce and, frankly, covering more than a corner of
the province in the ten days allowed seemed a physical
impossibility.

I suggested to Mr Ahmed that we split up. He was the senior member of the team so I thought it would be proper if he followed the Government in its campaign. I would take the Opposition, and I had already noticed that Mr Chiluba, the Opposition Leader, was having his major rally in Northern Province. Why did we not find a second vehicle and driver? After two days of bouncing around with me Mr Ahmed saw sense. We achieved the impossible in finding another car – a much more comfortable vehicle – and he went off in style with a second driver, looking as if he were an administrator in the Indian Empire. Always smiling, neatly dressed and tidily equipped with pen and paper.

We split up the map between us, according to where the meetings were being held and I tracked Mr Chiluba and his colleagues with growing excitement. For, politically, this election was of large importance indeed. As I got under the surface I discovered that President Kaunda had done all he could to narrow the voting register in order to exclude the young, who almost all opposed him. Twenty-year-old girls, plump, shy and dimpling, said that they had been told in school that only those over twenty-one years of age were allowed to register. They had also been told that they could not take time off from school to go to the registration office in any case. On top of that, the register had only been opened for ten days once in seventeen years, the previous November. Actually, the voting age was eighteen and all the upper formers of schools should have been given time off and encouraged to put their names forward. Other people had been told that they did not qualify for different and equally invalid reasons.

The international community thought that the country was in such turmoil that the elections would be violent and bloody. They foresaw that the President would win (his power was, after all, total and his bow to democracy a brief one) and they feared for the safety of the few staff that they had in the provinces as well as in Lusaka. They

called their expatriates back to base and flew many of
them out of the country. The country's tension grew
sharply in the last few days before the vote, when the
President of the Bank of Zambia was seen boarding a
flight to Harare, and rumour had it that the national
reserves were stored in sacks in the hold of his aeroplane. People said that the country's wealth had been
withdrawn in anticipation of a revolution.

I felt that a revolution was unlikely. Going from village
to village, talking with hundreds of people, I found deep
happiness at being allowed to vote. Their satisfaction
at having foreign Observer teams was very great. They
believed, and I think rightly, that our presence and
President Carter's team's presence also was a key determinant in ensuring a free and fair election. President
Carter's team was indeed an interesting one. Their public
relations were magnificent. The noise and furore that
they created of their coming was superlative in size and
quality. In fact, they were a very small group of people
in a hotel room in Lusaka, collating statistics and setting
up a system whereby the vote would be analysed very
stringently after it had been taken. I personally could
not see how this could make the election itself any fairer
but none the less I saw that it was an interesting activity
in its own right and could be used subsequently were the
election a flop democratically. Their monitoring teams as
such did not arrive until the day of the election. I found
one team wandering in the back streets of Kasama at the
end of a long night, with two of them asking plaintively
exactly where they were and what was happening. It
didn't matter; their work had been done by the publicity
machine and this put the fear of international disapproval
into Kaunda's supporters.

Travelling hundreds of miles along the dusty lanes of
Northern Province showed me how corrupt Kaunda's
Government had become. The small farmers, in terms
of desperation, told me that the Government was the
compulsory purchaser and therefore transported all their

produce. However, the Government lorries did not turn up any longer although farmers were still ordered to put their millet sacks on the side of the road to await the transport. The sacks of millet rotted by the roadside and the trucks never came. I saw the sacks of ruined grain piled high. The farmers had no income as a result of Government corruption and mismanagement.

Thus the Chiluba final election campaign meeting was a brave demonstration of a nation's desperation for change. The confidence of people in the strength of 'one man, one vote' was total. The tales told of methods used to undermine a person's choice of where to put their vote were many (bribery, distortion of election processes, the make-up of the register). The fears of the loss or deliberate replacement of ballot boxes once they were locked and sealed were in the forefront of people's worries. And, as the vast field filled and spread with people, walking for days with carried children, I asked the heavily armed police, counting at the entry gates, for an assessment of the numbers present. Ten thousand plus, they said, and more to come. Several hours later, in the heat of the midday sun, Chiluba's tiny plane circled above and landed. Deep-voiced singing and swaying masses greeted him, arms out to touch him as he, slight and slender, with visionary dignity, was squeezed through the crowds and on to the platform. He beckoned me to join him and asked me to speak. I gave a brief statement on the Commonwealth Observer team's mission of electoral fairness and how we were carrying out our work. Great cheers of thankfulness and encouragement came welling up. Then Chiluba spoke and the field was engulfed in waves of sound supporting him. On election day, starting at 5 a.m., I toured polling booths in schools and village meeting places, checking and checking again. Mr Ahmed did the same, a hundred miles away. One bush polling booth was filled with Government supporters, who were guiding voters to the voting booth and leaning over their shoulders to indicate where to mark. By then the police were very good friends of mine. I sent for a fresh contingent to replace the local man who could not handle the powerful forces against him. The new men, a team in para-military gear with helmets and machine-guns, greeted me warmly, cleared the room politically and settled in for the duration. I heard later that that particular village was known for its corruption of any system. Elsewhere, electoral commission honesty was transparent in most places. And the feeling was optimistic, not necessarily that change would happen (the power of the State was known) but that the election was being properly overseen by independent, knowledgeable people who would make large noises internationally if the election was deemed to have been unfairly run.

The electoral climax was long-drawn-out as the collection of ballot boxes, with the vast distances and lack of transport, took many days. I travelled with several boxes guarded by soldiers. The counting hall was first filled with noise and shouts of excitement and, as the night wore on, with sleep. Young soldiers nodded off completely, leaning on guns and ammunition. They were not needed; the Kaunda party ceded defeat as the piles of votes for Chiluba's candidates heaped higher and higher. The final, national vote was over three-quarters for him.

I saw the new President Chiluba the next day, his first visitor after he came to power. Together we worked that morning and afternoon to find and release a vanished political prisoner, the missing witness of the Winnie Mandela case. Once found he told the President and myself that he saw Winnie stab Stompie herself. He looked like a man risen from the dead, pale-faced and thin, dressed in the next-door prisoner's pyjamas. South African-based UK journalist, the eminent Fred Bridgeland, had set me on that trail.

Zambia's election was over. With no revolution for international news consumption, the media people left. The national decline into acute poverty has continued, and Chiluba has declared political emergency steps, the sort that Kaunda started by taking so many years before. I recall his immediate concern for the political prisoners I identified for him eighteen months earlier. Is he another good man downed by political ill fortune? Is freedom in Africa only sustained by international attention? Can only the media spotlight ensure that African democracy lasts? And, since their job is to catch our attention, how can we not forget?

4

Out of India

After my mother died I went to India. Her death, after many months of suffering, left our whole family in the depths of loss and dejection. Her courage left us drained. Christmas 1971 without her was a bleak affair and I went afterwards to India to shake off my acute sadness by plunging myself into a new culture. I was also curious to see if the poverty for which India was renowned was as deep and grave as the reports made it sound.

On top of that, apart from seeing Indian friends I had the goal of reaching the equivalent school to my own St Mary's, Wantage, a carbon copy that the nuns themselves had run for over a hundred years in Poona. So the purpose of my mission was clear; to get to the Sisters and to enhance their work in whatever way I could, however minimally. I wanted to share their experiences, to match up the reality of their world with the clear picture I had had of them from the time when, as a child at school in Wantage, I had raised my first funds for overseas aid to help buy a buffalo for milk for the orphaned children the Sisters cared for.

India absorbed me totally and I was swept into her 4,000-year-old civilisation. My Sikh friends and other contacts in New Delhi were welcoming and I had superficial fun and excitement while absorbing the sounds, smells, noises and colours. Their thoughtfulness enabled me to keep my sorrow with me but also allowed it to diminish gently while the largeness that was India swirled around me.

India's Janus stance (looking both ways and being respectful of the past) was wonderfully expressed early one morning outside my window in Delhi. A wooden wheeled cart, dragged by two oxen, and carrying sacks of grain for market, approached a major crossroads. A tank leading a line of tanks drove up to the crossroads from another road. The cart-driver did not look up or stop and I feared for his safety. The soldier ordered his tanks to stop and the cart with oxen and driver plodded through.

Eventually, and leaving behind the social round, I went by train to Bombay. To get to know a country it is always better to travel alone. The train journey from Delhi to Bombay was a splendid experience. I went fourth class, the cheapest as I had no money, and talked with everyone along the route. India is a perfect country to explore alone. There is so much inquisitive friendliness that conversations start very easily indeed. Added to which, most people have some grasp of English as this is one of the two official languages throughout the forty-two states. So I was lucky in my choice of civilisation and I chattered happily all the way down and listened to the people in the carriages. It was a great squash as fourth class means almost nothing at all by way of comfort with just a wooden plank to sit on. Nearly the whole of India seemed to be sitting on the same plank as myself in our cramped and confined compartment.

I tumbled out in Bombay, grimy, drenched with sweat in the heat of the spring but very happy. I plucked up the courage (hotels in India are a little chancy) and went to the best hotel for two nights. It was called the Taj Mahal and was by the sea, overlooking the port. After I had checked in I overheard a large citizen of the United States of America, who was staring up from a guidebook, complaining bitterly to the manager. It was a heated altercation and I drew close to hear the American claiming that the guidebook had got it wrong, and the hotel was nothing like the description. As I listened further I choked with laughter. The manager caught my eye as we realised together that the American had identified the great Taj Mahal – the white marbled tomb in Agra of Shah Jehan's beautiful wife – as the hotel. It was Noël Coward brought to life, and was a reminder that it is very difficult to try to grasp the elements of a culture and people without historical or linguistic grounding. Without even a superficial understanding of a society efforts on aid become insulting.

I wandered around Bombay a little bit the following day and met with a coachload of North American elderly citizens, mostly women. They were angry too; and I asked why. They said they were 'doing India in two days' as part of a world tour and that they felt it was so very like the other places that they had visited. Were not all Hiltons the same everywhere and with nothing to choose between them? What was so different about India? They added the splendid comment that the tour route was very misleading too in that they had been told it would include Europe but in fact left out the United Kingdom. And 'Gee,' said one lady wonderingly, 'it said Yurrup, and if Britain ain't a part of Yurrup where is it?' As a strong European I was tempted to agree with her but did not wish to fan the flames between her and the tour courier which were already fierce.

The real reason for her angry despair emerged; she could not see how poverty and happiness could co-exist. She had seen some local people laughing and smiling, and since they were poor she found that inexplicable. She had reversed the inaccurate but widely held belief that wealth always brings happiness, and held a similar untrue view of poverty. The capacity of the human spirit to triumph over tragedy is something I have witnessed around the world. Neither poverty nor wealth need be determinants.

I wandered up to see the place of death for Zoroastrians, known as the Place of Silence, at the top of a high hill. The garden was walled off as it was here that the dead bodies were laid out and the vultures did their work of helping to return the corpses to earth and sea, to sky and fire. I fell into conversation with those nearby and discussed their faith. In their view, Christianity was a faulty creed since it created a duality in man, setting one part of him against the other through the internal identification of both good and evil. How could we be at peace inside ourselves, they asked, with that incessant war? I argued that such an easy way out ignored the complexities and illuminations of God's creations.

The Zoroastrians in Bombay are also called the Parsees, after their origins in Persia. The story goes that with the invasion of Persia in the fifteenth century by the Mongols, one group of Zoroastrians fled to India. They were not allowed to stop in any place as India was so full of people. They were sped on their way down the great subcontinent until, tired and exhausted, they reached Bombay. Desperate to stay they sought an interview with the local chieftain, who told them that the area was too crowded already and he would not allow them to settle down. As a last chance the leader of the Persians asked for a pitcher of milk, which was provided. He had it topped up until the milk reached the very brim of the jug. Then, calling for the local chief's attention, he pulled a silver coin out and said, watch, watch. Carefully he slipped in the coin, laying it flat, just tipping over the rim of the jug. The coin sank deep into the milk leaving not a ripple behind it. There, he said, see how my people will enter this place and settle among you if you let us do so. We will leave not a trace and you will not notice that we are here. Touched by his plight and by the ingenuity of his plea the chief allowed them to settle. The Parsees have flourished in Bombay ever since.

Later that day I went to some caves outside the city to view the paintings. I met with a family of Jains, that extreme form of gentle Hinduism which takes such trouble to avoid hurting anyone that its adherents walk by looking at the ground so as to avoid treading on any insect. They were a quiet group of mother, father and two children. We sat together on a bus and talked for a long time about their personal beliefs. Despite the difficulties it gave them (their method of eating is another problem) they feel so passionately about the duty to avoid giving pain to any living creature that they will go to all lengths to ensure that they themselves will not transgress. It is a very onerous religion, but before we dismiss it totally, what religion followed scrupulously is not? But the question remains: does the formatting and pursuit of the pathway to God so take up all our energies that we have no time left to *serve* God?

The history of constant religious strife is not far away in India, with the great wars between Muslims and Hindus. I, however, was looking for the Christian community in the back streets of Poona so I bade farewell to my Parsee, Hindu and Jain friends whom I had so briefly got to know in Bombay and set out on a little train for Poona. Tiny in comparison to the great express into Bombay, none the less it travelled a long way. On arrival in Poona I found a rickshaw and was carried into the poorest area of town.

For the first time in India I felt a little alone as the enormity of real poverty displayed itself. This was a vastly different society from the cosmopolitan riches and variety of Bombay, a different world from the tourist attractions of Agra and the Taj Mahal, a long way in every sense from the ordered, national capital of New Delhi and from the large sophistication and developed economy of the rich Punjab with its Chandigarh and the Golden Temple, its fertile lands stretching up to the disputed border with Pakistan. Perhaps the back of Poona is the more ordinary India and its poverty the life that most of India has to put up with every day and night.

St Mary's, Wantage, Poona version, proved a haven of Western values wrapped up in Indian dress. A small number, just a handful of elderly Anglican nuns, ran projects of the size that in Britain would have demanded ten times more staff. They commanded, with gentle and dedicated firmness, a band of helpers who were themselves all victims of the same poverty and physical ill health and disability that characterised the Poona needy. The difference was that within the loving framework that the Christian community offered, individual difficulties shrank in the sufferer's perception. Most importantly to me, victims became *controllers* of their lives and not recipients of misfortune. This is an important difference with the West which I believe we can learn a great deal from. So often in our own sincere forms of caring we actually make the sufferer powerless and impotent – a Western export which I believe passionately we must not engage in as part of our well-meaning aid.

The practical set-up was large. First there was the boarding school, which I went round immediately. This was for girls and the modest fees paid by their parents (the well-to-do crowd) helped to subsidise the remaining and numerically much larger work for the really poor and desperate. Here is another practical idea which other projects could adopt.

Many of the girls' parents were in the Indian equivalent of Sandhurst. This vast training centre for officers of all three forces of the Indian military command lay about fifty miles away in the plains of Poona. We visited there by courtesy of a friendship of the Mother Superior with the parents of one of the girls. It had all the space that the British Army struggles to find on Dartmoor and Salisbury Plain, in Norway, Germany and the Falklands. There was space much further than the eye could see for all the training exercises any army could wish to carry out. Airspace too was easy to find; there was no need for the British-style protests from the local residents against low-flying aircraft, nor the acute pressures of flight paths into Heathrow and Gatwick. Even the navy had a patch of water on which to play. The Wantage Sisters were the beggars, however, as those engaged in looking after the untouchables in India would be. Our approach to see even just a corner of this wonderland of efficiency and activity (quite unlike the remainder of India) was humble indeed!

The similarity of the boarding school to the sister school in Wantage was uncanny. The same Sister must have exercised her full responsibility for the economies in scale of purchasing, by buying identical goods and chattels for Poona as she did for Wantage in the early 1900s or so. There were the same blue serge curtains, drawn round each berth and at every window. There were the same individual hanging cupboards and little chests of drawers. Even the bedsteads were identical. I felt at one with all those girls who for one hundred years and more had been schooled in Poona just as I and countless others had been schooled in Wantage by the quiet dedication and steadfast vision of the nuns.

Naturally, Chapel was just the same as ours had been in school. The bell of the angelus swung clear-toned at 6 a.m., 12 noon, and 6 p.m. again and we stopped for prayer. The nine offices which the nuns carried out each day in addition to all their teaching and caring duties were fulfilled devotedly. The procession into Chapel was much smaller in Poona than it had been in Wantage. The whole order numbered 450 Sisters world-wide (there was another mission in southern Africa). In the convent and at school in Wantage a long line of black figures walked in close discipline and individual prayerful concentration into Chapel and dived swiftly into their Victorian copies of medieval monks' thrones. This shrank in Poona to a small procession in tropical white robes.

Coming out of the Poona boarding school, as the last step fell away from my heel I was back on the red earth of India where everything was different. Beggars with no legs or no arms, hauling themselves on crutches or being pushed on trolleys, chased me across the street bellowing for money. Children, perhaps blinded by their parents in order to become better beggars, shouted for support. Sad-faced women in rags from the caste of the untouchables shrank against the mud walls, appealing silently for recognition.

Perhaps most alien of all in these surroundings were the Anglo–Indian down-and-outs, whose shaded European features or way of walking struck a different tone immediately. They were despised by everyone. They were the write-offs of two democratic nations, each signatories to the United Nations Declaration of Human Rights, one of which (the United Kingdom) had drafted the Declaration of the Rights of the Child, and the other of whom (India) was so proud that she would only accept money to relieve the poverty of her nation and kept out Western voluntary workers.

For the nuns of Wantage were not permitted to bring in other Sisters since this was seen as a missionary activity. As they grew older they could not be replaced. Thus the old Sisters never took home leave as they knew they would not be permitted to return to their beloved India. They would have to cease helping the orphans and the old people, some younger than themselves, on whom they poured out their practical version of the love of God. National pride, a stance adopted by civil servants and politicians who lived comfortably, endangered help for India's poor, I thought.

All over the world it is the smell of poverty that betrays its presence. People's inability to find a place to put their excrement is the beginning of the stench. There is generally no place for rubbish either and for most of the really poor the rubbish of others will be a resource through which they trove for daily sustenance and shelter. Many a group of people live on waste-disposal sites, that is on rotting rubbish dumps of city refuse. There they trawl endlessly for pieces of corrugated iron (a real find), cardboard and sack wrappings and scraps of clothing. They grub for ends of discarded food on which to live, scraping the bottoms of tins and wrappings. Even away from the rubbish dumps, poverty breeds rats and cockroaches, great scuttling black things, both of them with all the filth and squalor that they bring. Then there is the stench of human sickness, ulcerated mouths, weeping eye infections, matting hair that never can be washed, with fleas and nits in plenty. Poverty stinks and it degrades a human being; the personal dignity given by cleanliness proves out of reach for the really poor.

The oddity about the Poona Wantage Sisters was their ability to make things clean on the slenderest resources. They are a wonderful example. The orphanage housed 2,000 children, many starving, from an unnoticed famine in a nearby province. Their despairing families placed them on the doorstep silently and left them there. The orphanage was small indeed and yet the children were squeaky clean. Quiet, like starving children often are, but lovingly cared for and hugged, not just by the nuns but by the helpers they had trained. Each child was shown how much it mattered as a child of God. Many of these helpers were elderly women who had been brought up in the orphanage themselves, had gone out to get married (the nuns were practical marriage brokers of a high order indeed), and had come back later in their lives to help the Sisters whom they loved nurse others in a situation similar to the one they had been in themselves in childhood.

These elderly ladies had retained the habits of childhood, instilled into them by the sisters: cleanliness, dedication, hard work, and still the commitment to worship whether as Christians or Hindus. For if the family of a resident (child or old person) was a Hindu the nuns were extremely cautious in seeking to convert them, knowing that the cost would rule out family reintegration if that became a reality.

That seems to me the ultimate in charity, the caritas, or caring that one human being can give another. To respect a person's religious beliefs and enhance their chances of fulfilling the best of talents or of standards that can be found within them shows real respect. These things were not discussed with me by the nuns, they took them for granted, but it was something that I saw and honoured fully in my thinking.

I slept in the orphanage in Poona. Because space was so limited my bed was only four foot long as it belonged to a child. I followed the Sisters around learning from them how they managed this vast portfolio of work with fun and cheerfulness, with competence and to the highest standards.

Next-door to the orphanage was the home for the elderly. There I found an equivalent home to the one I knew so well in Wantage called St Katharine's Home. St Katharine's Home, Wantage, was next-door to St Mary's School and of an evening or on a Saturday more senior girls were allowed to go and sit with the elderly ladies. They came from impoverished backgrounds and needed care. Many an hour I had spent in St Katharine's Home, Wantage, when in the sixth form at school and studying A levels. If I closed my eyes in Poona and listened to the chatter, I felt I was in St Katharine's once more. Discipline, cheerfulness, plenty of good works in terms of knitting and sewing and weaving to create goods for other people even less fortunate than those in the home, these were identical here in Poona to the projects still going on in St Katharine's Home.

The difference lay in the fact that in St Katharine's Home lived the Wantage Overseas Secretary, Sister Cora, a tiny birdlike lady with complicated teeth and a large smile displaying her lack of dental care in childhood. Her task was to keep track of all those who gave to support the Order's work in Poona. Here I was seeing the results of her steady application to her task.

A modest recruiting effort, so low-key that the authorities could not frown upon it, resulted in more Sisters joining the community from the local population. A large handful of younger women had been professed and were now serving in all-white habits as full Sisters. They talked of the pride and joy of Mother Superior's existence, her ashram. This was the controversial multi-faith place of worship that she had created, to find ways of praying and honouring God and goodness with the outside non-Christian community without altering the tenets of the religions involved.

In stark contrast, further down the road there was a notorious ashram which subsequently moved to California and in the 1980s was broken up by the police and the drugs removed and Rolls-Royces redistributed. That was unlike our ashram, which was the real thing. Indeed, it was so innovative that permission had to be sought for its existence at the highest level.

Since the Anglican nuns had twinned up with some Catholic nuns from Belgium and with the local Hindu priests and a Muslim to form the ashram, this meant that both the Archbishop of Canterbury and the Pope had to give their written permission for shared Masses and other offices to be held. I went at once to Mass there, both to worship and to discover the reason for the fuss. It was clear at once that both the Archbishop and the Pope had been right to question and yet to endorse the project. Formal Mass was carried out by two priests (Anglican and Catholic) sharing the service with a Hindu, who brought in selected readings from the Hindu writings. Philosophical thoughts from the Guru Granth Sahib were inserted in place of prayers normally found within the Mass. The essential Catholic Prayer of Consecration remained. But even that was said by the priest kneeling within a Hindu circle on the floor and drawing Hindu symbols. The congregation came from all three religious paths. The service was said early in the morning, just after sunrise, and all the doors were open. The Indian sun streamed in, paler than it would be later in the day but still strong enough to strike the colours of the chalk marks on the floor and make the dust circle dance.

While our shared closeness of worship to God seemed very rich, this was a large and radical departure from normal Christian practice. I learned much spiritually from it. Firstly, it was clear that their shared cross-faith worship was a high-risk activity spiritually. The most acute danger was that the gold, silver and scarlet threads of single faiths would not be woven by the worshippers into an offering to God with each colour shining brightly and individually, but would end up as a tangled, knotted skein, reflecting human failure. Secondly, it was an activity that could readily be misunderstood and misrepresented by others. Thirdly, it could lead people away from God if they were not willing to explore faith very deeply. It could offer a shallow, muddled pathway.

On the plus side, if the experiment (for it was one) was stringently monitored and reviewed it offered a unique insight into other faiths and gave a unique opportunity to share worship across historic, often bloody, borders. I concluded that this was like lightning, a rare form of exciting illumination to be treated with extreme caution.

Sikh friends in Delhi and the Punjab had been unhappy at my coming further south and travelling without them. They were concerned lest I should get 'the wrong idea' of India. Letters came down asking me to go back and leave the poor. This strengthened my certainty that the poor were ninety per cent of India and that therefore this was where I belonged.

The final part of the Sisters' work, apart from the day school for girls (just like St Helen's, Abingdon) was their fund-raising activities. Despite the support from Britain they had to work hard in unpromising surroundings to keep their work financially afloat. It was a little like a large mushroom resting upon a slender, single stalk of finance. Without just a little money, the work would collapse. But even a small donation would make a large difference to a child's life through the Sisters' economy of style. A crisis was triggered by famine. Children were brought and left on the doorstep of the orphanage in hundreds from the next-door state. I accompanied the Sister Superior and her deputy to Bombay to help her search for money. She knew some wealthy families and

I gave her introductions to some others. People were generous to us, particularly the Parsees.

On my eventual return to the United Kingdom I took out a child sponsorship and encouraged others to do the same through Wantage Overseas, whose sponsorship programme paid continually for the education of individual children. My present child, Vasha, is doing wonderfully well. Her father was a labourer and died of cancer when she was two, her mother, being left with several children and no means of supporting them turned to the Sisters for help. Vasha is now turned thirteen and passing her exams each year successfully.

The kaleidoscope of India fell away behind me as the aeroplane flew out of Bombay. My money had run out (I could not work in India as a visitor and nor would I have wished to have taken work away from such intelligent people who could so ably perform every task themselves, and were eager to do so). So I had written to my father, just a brief note, saying that I had run out of funds. I had expected him to send me perhaps another £250, even if only as a loan. I reckoned without paternal desperation. Reading my letters from Poona, particularly, and smelling from them his own love of the subcontinent, he became fearful I might stay there for life, either as a nun or missionary or just as a Westerner absorbed into the alleviation of poverty. For once, therefore, my father let me down. He wrote back to me in India: 'Darling Emma, it will be nice to see you again.'

But, in fact, I had learnt much in four months there. My stay had been long enough to reaffirm for ever the knowledge that earthly possessions do not matter in the battle for recognition of self-worth. The patterning of God in mankind is sufficient reason for valuing ourselves and others and for pricing ourselves and others at the highest level. And I had learned again of the long haul in the battle to change poverty to happier times for others. India's rich were resistant to change: did they need the poor and the caste system to enhance their own difference? Individuals should not need degradation of others to feed their own importance. Could not God take that part for them?

My father had known India since 1946, when as a young Member of Parliament he and Arthur Bottomley – the Labour Member who subsequently became a Labour Government Colonial Office Secretary – went there to do a preliminary report for the House of Commons on the difficult question of Indian independence. They spent three months in India. In order to test out the real feelings of the Indians they slipped their handlers and went outside the cities and spent their time wandering in villages and asking people's opinions. They came back convinced that ordinary Indians wished for independence. They had presented a report to that effect at the House of Commons, which became the trigger for the subsequent political work on independence which came in 1947.

Arthur Bottomley became my honorary godfather as a result and I still tease him on his famous spoonerism with my father. Arthur was notorious for swapping names in his mind and bringing out the wrong one. He and my father had the final and most important meeting of their trip with Gandhi. In they walked and Arthur Bottomley stuck out his hand. 'Good morning, Mr Jinnah,' he said happily, naming the Opposition Leader to Gandhi's party. I had last seen Arthur in Zambia in 1964 when, at independence celebrations there, he did the same thing again. At the formal banquet he got up and addressed the assembled company as 'My noble Gambians'. His warmth is endless and his love for others infinite.

I did not return to India for nearly twenty years. Contact with Indian voluntary organisations remained constant and the funds that I have helped to raise in consequence for the pursuance of their work has been large too. Standing beside a field in southern India in 1991 and looking at the ten-year-old girls slaving away, weeding and harvesting under their parents' eyes,

I wondered if education could supplant poverty more quickly than shared worship. I recognised the wealth of inherited thoughtfulness that lies within each Indian child and the short life of intellectual development they are allowed. They receive free primary schooling but then without extra income the families are forced to take them out to work. Work for children in the fields accompanying their parents is standard practice and leads to a life expectancy of forty-five years or so. Work as a child prostitute is perhaps less ordinary but still very common in the big cities, where children are on their own.

The problem for the parents is a financial one. Apart from the loss of potential child earnings, it takes money to get to secondary school, just as it does in every developing country in the world. Although the lessons may be free there are books to be bought, pencils and rubbers and pens to be acquired, lunch to be purchased and transport to be paid for too. The cumulative effect is financially so large that little progress for the world's poorest children can be made in terms of education unless new, non-parental income can be found.

It is difficult to raise money, save by sponsorship, for educating Third World children. But child sponsorship has become unpopular in much of the professional, charitable field because of the personalisation it involves. Many professional workers now strongly advocate an anonymity of recipient. A result of that policy is less commitment from the West as a sea of needy faces without names becomes a crowd whose needs we can down grade more easily. Often, it seems more attractive emotionally for the West to pile up trucks in Britain with tins of battered tomato soup and boxes full of second-hand clothing. The resultant expense of driving the goods overland, shipping them overseas and landing and redistributing in the area of need is large for the donor. The money spent and the energy would most often have been put to better use by helping meet the education needs of early teenage children. Only then could they themselves as adults be able to help to change the plight of those below them on the ladder of poverty. If we want to help others, we must cease using them to pay back our own emotional or spiritual debts.

5

The Role of Aid

Working in the Save The Children Fund identified and sometimes solved some of the difficulties of developing-country work and of the non-governmental organisation world. My aim in joining was to return to India. On my return from India to the UK I had been offered two important jobs, one by IBM and one by the large consulting group, PE. On top of that, my kindly boss, Philip Richardson, at the Southwark Street partnership where I had a good job as a management consultant, had kept my job open while I had been away. He knew of my mother's illness and death, and of the strains that this had caused me.

I had also investigated the possibility of reading Comparative Religion at King's College, London. I could not get a grant, however, and in the interview I discovered that the basis for the course was wholly Christian. Although the Dean assured me that it was important to start with one religion and compare the others with that, it seemed too biased an approach. This would not satisfy my continuing desire to explore the differences between and similarities of the religions of the world.

I also wondered about being a social worker, but a visit to Westminster Social Services department made me conclude at once that their style of work was too imprecise and unquantifiable for me. Their thinking was not vigorous enough to fit my pattern of work and I could

The author, aged 6.

Above:
This camp at Shustar, Khozistaan Province in southern Iran, is home to thousands of Iraqi refugees.

Right:
A makeshift classroom without a single book.

Right:
This woman was forced to watch her husband executed by being run down by a line of tanks.

Centre right:
Will she see her home again? A refugee camp child.

Below:
Childhood joy survives in tragedy inside a refugee camp.

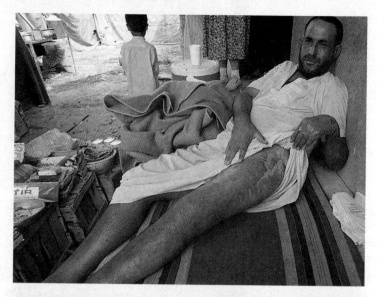

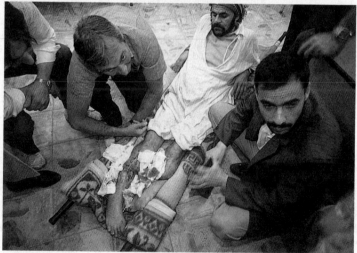

Top: A napalm bomb victim. The wound reaches to the bone and will not heal.

Above: A recent victim of a Basra mine, later operated on by Tony Rowsell.

Facing page: Sadness with a wealth of memories for an Iraqi Shi'ite refugee on the Iranian border.

Left:
In Search of a homeland - these refugees from the Iraqi marshes have made their homes on the Iranian border.

Right:
Food and water is brought to this child by friends of the Amar appeal.

Above: A professional family from Basra forced to flee their own country.

Below: Inside the marshes.

Right:
Sheik Hammoodi
with Archbishop
Carey at Lambeth
Palace, May 1993.

Below:
Michael teaches
Amar chess (the
game his ancestors
invented).

not find satisfactorily firm goals and targets against which I assumed they were measuring their workload.

Why then choose the Save The Children Fund? Simply because in the front of my mind was the suffering I had seen in India. I hoped to go back to add to the work I had done so far. All the aid efforts there were wholly insufficient in the face of India's vast need. What did the large voluntary organisations see as effective ways of conquering poverty? How did they try to sow the seeds of long-term, sustainable prosperity for the world's children, in particular? It was a worthwhile topic to explore. Maybe they had some secular answers to add to the Wantage portfolio of proven work.

My first task in the Save The Children Fund was nothing to do with India. The new computer had failed; help was indeed urgently needed, but sensitivity too. For the staff of eminent financial notables on the Finance Committee had made a bad business decision. It was wholly understandable. With a charity that ran on such economical lines the lowest tender for this new and vastly expensive piece of equipment seemed the right one to accept. By a freak ill chance the company they chose was in financial straits and worse.

In the computer room a group of contract programmers were working. But on inspecting their worksheets it became clear that, while they had been hired to carry out the Save The Children's work, they were working on projects for other clients. They were cheating the Save The Children Fund. It took some time, however, to persuade my new colleagues that this was so. They found it extraordinarily difficult to believe that they were being conned on such a major scale. Who would treat a voluntary organisation so shabbily?

At one point the Bank of England secondee, six-foot tall and white-haired, Hugh Excell, took me aside and told me seriously that if I kept on saying how bad the computer company was I would drive them into bankruptcy. Unfortunately, they were indeed bad. An article in the *Investors Chronicle* stated that the German police had a warrant out for the arrest of the directors of the company. They had cheated a client once too often in the Federal Republic of Germany.

The other worry the Finance Department had was that once the Save The Children Fund governing council discovered the scale of the error, jobs would be at risk. But it became clear that the company was indeed a rogue elephant. No one could be blamed. The task was to smooth over the edges as fast as possible and get the system back on track with a different supplier of equipment. My three weeks of employment (a personal forecast) stretched into thirteen months. IBM and PE faded into the past. Comparative religion went on hold. The work for India was on my agenda still but in a different way. It became clear that business and information technology skills were as instrumental in assisting the problems of the developing world and the poor in the United Kingdom, as were the skills of the medical profession or of the aid distributors. I spent the next few years working to improve the administration and fund-raising aspects of Save The Children. The task was to administer the work well and raise the money with maximum economy.

The real difficulty in fund-raising is how to harness resources effectively, particularly if they are voluntary. It is easy to spend time and energy and involve half a million people on a fruitless initiative that raises practically no funds. On the other hand, with extreme skill it is possible to raise a million pounds with no expenditure other than personal energy. The topic of money took on a new importance. It really mattered for thousands of children depending on fund-raising efforts.

The Finance Department was full of wonderful allies. The Chief Accountant, Tim Phipps, rose to be Financial Director and then Deputy Director. He was a Shrewsbury public-school boy, enormously talented and wholly committed to the cause of needy children. His soft heart was well encased in a financial strait-jacket. He was a nightmare at budget time, particularly for fund-raisers. In an emergency, however, he was a real friend. Maybe he normally saw fund-raisers as an irritant, and felt that somehow the money should flow in without them. None the less, he did not question too closely the source of £18,500 I handed to him in greasy, used pound notes. (It was a result of a pop concert by an American star who had already crossed the Atlantic back to his home base in California and would not have paid UK tax.) Tim Phipps was less forgiving with the salary curtailment of a lady who was misguidedly taken on in the direct mail department. She took a lot of sick leave in her first three weeks of employment. Workmates were kind at first. It became a different story when she was found outside the front door plying the oldest trade of all, and not even giving the proceeds back to the Save The Children Fund.

Tim Phipps' deputy, the mild-mannered, always smiling, Irish charmer Mike Regan became and has remained a lifelong friend and colleague. He and I work now on cancer relief, Iraqi children and Romanian children. Mike's Irish warmth reflects the best of Eire. Air Commodore Hibbert was the Deputy Director General in 1974. I called him a flight sergeant in error in my first week and nearly lost my job. Only the knowledge that no one else could solve the computer problem saved me.

The Chairman of the Welsh Council, Lady Williams, had jet-black hair and white, fine skin. Her family had come over with the Spanish Armada. An advertising agency once tried to sell its services to the Save The Children Fund on the grounds that they were the Government's Family Planning authority. Lady Williams demolished them with the immortal words: 'You aren't very successful are you? There are far too many unwanted children alive.'

The *grande dame* of all was Lady Alexandra Metcalfe, the daughter of a Viceroy of India (the job my grandfather did not take up). She was wedded to the concept of public service from her youth in Delhi. She travelled widely at her own expense, saw children in despair and came back with ideas and wonderful new initiatives. She sat as Council Member for thirty years or more. She and caretaker Mrs Clark, the former housekeeper of Miss Jebb, represented the two financial extremes of the Save The Children Fund. One was rich and one poor, but both worked unselfishly for those they deemed to be in greater need.

Ursula Sheridan was Chairman of the 800 voluntary Branches. These groups carried out classical British fund-raising work. Ursula had been sent to the UK by her parents from Eastern Europe as the Second World War broke out. Her family died in concentration camps. (One of her daughters became the second woman rabbi in the UK.) Joan Marten, wife of the Conservative Member of Parliament Neil Marten, was also a Branches and a Council Member. Her husband later became Minister for Overseas Development, the ODA, and she persuaded him to initiate the pound-for-pound grant, which became a staple of British Government support for voluntary organisations running overseas projects. Nigel Fisher, another Conservative Member of Parliament, came on the Council and proved to be a strong provider of good ideas. Mrs Callaghan, Jim Callaghan's wife, was another independent and prominent member. Robert Rhodes James MP was later involved too.

But how was the money raised in the name of the Save The Children Fund actually spent? My first boss, Patricia Bryden, had sent me to see a project so that I could see the work in action. As economy was at that time important for the Save The Children Fund, I went to see the work relatively nearby in Agadir and Khemisset, near Fès, Morocco.

In Agadir, the Save The Children Fund at that time ran a day school for polio and spina bifida victims. There was also a school for the blind. A father came in crying and saying to the project director, Bridget Stevenson, in

Arabic, 'Oh Allah, why is it that my blind son is being educated? I do not understand it, this is the one who is blind and yet he is the one who is able to read and write and the children who are sighted cannot. How can Allah explain this?'

The day school in Agadir was an astonishing sight, with hundreds of children getting off minibuses with crutches and callipers, and carrying out a full school day. It was matched by the boarding school for even needier children in Khemisset, where children with drastic polio injuries from families with no money at all learnt in simple surroundings how to conquer their handicap and pass the baccalaureate. Both schools had workshops in which the older pupils were taught by carpenters to make the callipers and crutches. Wooden planks were sawn up and small legs measured for supporting splints for limbs that had withered to the size of a sapling. With these aids the schools' football teams flourished. But in spite of all these efforts, polio was a crippling disease that bore down very heavily in poorer countries. How could it be conquered? There seemed no possibility of the drastic international activity needed. I triggered it as the new Fund Raising Director.

The Stop Polio campaign came as a result of Treasurer Edward Pollitzer's constant niggling. Way back in 1977 he started badgering our department about the coming sixtieth anniversary in 1979. He felt that it should be an opportunity for new initiatives for fund-raising. He wanted us to start planning for some huge and time-consuming celebratory event. He was right, but we felt that he would not be doing the hard work that would be required to make anything effective happen. None the less, he had his way and we put together a committee to think up fund-raising ideas for celebration. We came up first with the idea of a classical garden party at which our patron HM The Queen might honour us. But that was surely not enough. I felt that what we really needed was a new project overseas, something to mark the anniversary by way of tribute through long-term work for the children whom we were trying to help. I wandered downstairs to the overseas department to suggest this and the Stop Polio campaign was born, an immunisation programme designed to reach out world-wide and to curtail, if not eliminate, that scourge of all mankind.

The first picture we used as a fund-raising illustration was of a polio case in Ancient Egypt. A drawing from a pyramid tomb showed the antiquity of the disease. We began the long haul towards possible eradication. The project was started in three small countries of southern Africa: Lesotho, Swaziland and Malawi. Polio was very widespread in all three places and under the guidance of Dr Nicholas Ward, recruited from the World Health Organisation, the programme steadily took shape. A governing board to raise the money and take an overview was created under the chairmanship of Robert Rhodes James, with Sir John Butterfield, then Dean of Cambridge, as the Deputy. The idea caught on and over a period of four years £10 million was raised by us world-wide with which Nick Ward and his team of colleagues set up and ran immensely successful pilot schemes. It was complex fund-raising; commitments had to be given not to deplete general funds since this would affect other work adversely. Nick and I planned to move on to Egypt and Morocco where polio was very widespread indeed and still is.

The Save The Children Fund had always had an immunisation component in their mother/child health-care programmes. The classical Save The Children programme in a developing-world country was centred on mobile health-care clinics. Long-wheel-based Land-rovers were the best vehicles since they went everywhere and, once these were equipped with drugs, nurses, stretchers and everything necessary for a health-care clinic on the move, the mother/child projects were initiated. I saw them in operation in Central America where, in the depths of the jungle, hundreds of women and children were waiting for the weekly visit of the Save The Children mobile health clinic.

The key to the success of the schemes was the training side. The field director's task was to be the initiator and negotiator with the national government and local authorities. Success for him or her lay in setting up the training component of a mother/child health-care project. The most important part of the project was to get government recognition of the qualification that a trainee health worker needed to practise health care. This ensured the continuation of the scheme long-term, since once a government had adopted a certification process then the qualified people were able to practise their new disciplines in their own village environment. Naturally, immunisation was a part of the mother/child health-care project.

What we were doing, therefore, in pulling out polio and in tackling the other five immunisations against childhood diseases on to the Stop Polio campaign was skewing the emphasis on to preventative medicine and away from curative. The trouble was that we became too successful, and the Stop Polio campaign started to dominate the work internationally. Certainly, it was a programme that became very widely known indeed. After several years the overseas department took the decision that other work had to predominate and the Stop Polio campaign should fade. Dr Nicholas Ward left and rejoined the World Health Organisation. Today, he heads the WHO Stop Polio campaign for the entire world as Head of the World Health Organisation preventative health-care programme in Geneva.

The work overseas, generally, was carried out and planned by a handful of the most remarkable people. Eileen Watson, red-haired and no longer young, was a Deputy Director for a long while of the overseas department. Her colleague and co-worker, Jerry Fonseca, of the sherry family, was a Deputy Director too and eventually took the prized position he hungered after,

Director of the overseas department. The first overseas director I knew was a quiet colonel, Tony Hawkins; he was succeeded by a former fieldworker from the Colonial Office, John Cumber, later Sir John when he became Director General. John's term of office coincided with a wonderful spurt that was achieved in fund-raising and he was therefore given the task of enlarging the Save The Children's work overseas by doubling it in size. He spent the best part of a year or two travelling, and identified and thought up some highly satisfactory projects, lifting the Save The Children number of fieldworking countries from about twenty-three to over forty.

The old Colonial Office had always provided first-rate people for the Save The Children Fund. A former colonial police commissioner, no less, Peter Owen, who held the Queen's Police medal awarded to him for personal bravery when he evacuated civilians under fire in Aden, became my fund-raising deputy. Peter had a gammy leg, a fall-out from his sporting years as a young police officer, a wide girth and a huge and smiling face. His professional way of assessing a situation was to tackle each problem as a unique one. He scorned the Army attitude, which was 'look up the rule book', according to him.

Mind you, that was a very helpful attitude as there were plenty of former Army officers in our fund-raising team and new policies and ideas were flowing. First-class people were needed to implement action. The competence and commitment of the majors and colonels provided the administration needed. And they knew what they were talking about. Poverty in the developing world was not a fantasy to them as it was to so many of our most dedicated supporters; it was a reality, and they could talk with the utmost sincerity grafted on to real knowledge, albeit from some time ago and often in a war zone.

The Colonial Office people were something different again. They had been able to take a rounder view of their particular territories. They knew their local people very well. They spoke the language and had learned the appropriate laws and customs. District Commissioners and Officers administered the legal system. They understood the different tribal and religious conflicts. They were thus able to bring a breadth of experience to their Save The Children work, derived from long years of service to HMG overseas.

Out in the field, Save The Children traditionally specialised in medical work. This was an eminently sensible decision since it is the least political and often the most necessary of work. Thus, overseas staff members were most often doctors or health workers. Community nurses were the staple of many long-term programmes. Primary health care did not need doctors (who were in any case expensive) and the community nurses were able to train others and work under a variety of trying circumstances without recourse to higher medical authority. Hospital nurses were a more sheltered breed.

Sponsorship of children's education, emergency and disaster work for families in greatest need and preventative and curative medicine for mothers and children were the major overseas programmes that Save The Children (UK) planned and implemented. Other members of the Save The Children international family specialised in leprosy control (the Danes) or community care (the USA). Sweden and Norway were other long-term family members. All of them felt the same pull between solving some of the needs in their own countries and responding to the far greater cry for help from the poor in India, Africa, Central and South America and the Far East. 'Charity begins at home' is a perennial reproach. Striking the balance between home and overseas work was difficult for the UK Save The Children Fund. Famines and floods in the developing world brought in the money that saved millions of lives, but children were in need in Britain, too.

The tensions between the work for children in the United Kingdom and work for children overseas grew

unexpectedly acute when we left our office in Queen
Anne's Gate and moved to Stockwell. Queen Anne's Gate
was a building lent to us at the tail end of a crown lease
for which we paid a peppercorn rent. This lease collapsed
and suddenly we had to move. We took over, and altered
to our specification, a drab building in Stockwell. It was
like being on the inside of a very large aeroplane hangar;
and had poor quality air-conditioning since the Council
decreed that too much money should not be spent on
staff. Many people suffered sore throats and eyes and
had to leave as a result. It was a short-sighted policy.
Staff conditions in a building directly affect health and
should be adequate.

At the same time we started to recruit a more challenging group of UK fieldworkers. These were the new
professionals, the social workers. They were determined
to make their work as prominent as that of the overseas
staff. This meant large changes which were difficult
to achieve. While it is possible to feature death and
starvation from, say, an earthquake on television, and
do it sensitively, dramatising children's needs in Britain
in the same stark terms is unrealistic, except for a few
individual children whom it would not be right to have
named. So the work itself had to be altered. Playgroups
and valuable hospital work for sick children almost
disappeared. Work with other disadvantaged groups,
with particular reference to ethnic and gypsy minorities
was enlarged. Save The Children took on a Government
agency role to settle Vietnamese orphans and refugees
from Hong Kong. This was a very high-profile activity
which led to conflict between internal and voluntary staff.
It was tough getting the social workers to see that they
belonged to the Save The Children Fund and not that the
Save The Children Fund belonged to them. Despite all the
difficulties, some interesting work was carried out, new
concepts developed, and new groups of children helped.
However, it did not lead to a happy ship, particularly
when the staff were led by the social workers to join the

trades union, ASTMS, and the Save The Children Fund President, Her Royal Highness The Princess Anne, was secondary-picketed on her visit to a project in Liverpool. Unionisation also brought a great uplift in salaries and accompanying benefits, such as company cars, on a scale that had not been available to staff before and had not previously been sought.

Questions of staff conditions were difficult to solve. The truth was that a culture of 'them and us' had grown up between some of the volunteers and some of the staff. It was difficult to tell which side thought that it was taking which role. Who decided policy, and who executed it? The lines were blurring. The feeling of partnership, so strong when the organisation was small and struggling, seemed to diminish and proved difficult to recapture.

Staff had to have adequate pay; but what was adequate, when those in need for whom the organisation existed had almost nothing? Fieldworkers of long-standing came in and scorned the growing comfort and ease of Head Office. They worked harder than us, for less pay and in traumatic conditions.

These stresses and strains were in some way an inevitable consequence of swift income growth. Maybe our fund-raising department was partly to blame for this since we worked hard to create innovative fund-raising that was appropriate to the children that we served. The income went up and outwards through the ceiling. The social workers gathered Government funding for work in Britain. The overseas department became close to the ODA and gained considerable benefit financially.

In 1973, the Save The Children Fund annual income was £3.2 million. Eleven years later, the annual income was £42 million. This vast leap was not accomplished without extraordinary efforts by all our staff and volunteers. It placed great stresses and strains on the accountability practised by the finance department (was it still correct for fund-raisers to say that every penny counted?), and of course the expenditure difficulties for

effective new work gave large problems to the overseas
and UK departments, staff and committees.

On the fund-raising side our information technology
knowledge grew and grew. One of the basic fund-raising
tools was the direct mail list. This was husbanded by Pam
Gerrard-Smith, who carried out the task for twenty years
or more. Under skilled hands the numbers swelled and
swelled again. Some in-house research suggested that
people were comfortable giving eight times a year if they
were properly approached. More copies of *The World's
Children* were dispatched and new and enticing letters
framed. The income increased in consequence.

Although fund-raising is work undertaken for a serious purpose, long faces generally raise little money.
Fund-raising can properly be light-hearted, although
not ostentatious. The establishment set up a special
events department. We were glad to gain the services
of Rosamond Wynn-Pope for this effort. Large, pale and
calm, she gathered in other friends and settled down to
devise a series of appropriate events which brought the
organisation first-class publicity and raised considerable
money.

Jane Reed, the imaginative editor of *Woman's Own*,
sponsored Jumbly in Olympia in a hall that was unexpectedly free. Twenty-five thousand people came to the
world's largest jumble sale and the police pointed out
that most of the crooks of London were among them.
Crime knew no charitable restraints. Half-way through
the morning our volunteers selling the twenty-five tons
of jumble on the stalls were in despair since money was
walking out faster in the pockets of thieves than was
being raised. The Army swiftly offered 100 off-duty volunteers. Tall and fit, they walked around sternly staring
down at everyone and looking particularly carefully at the
tills. The pilfering stopped. The second day was marred
only by a strike by the union who ran Olympia. Norman
Willis of the TUC (by then a friend) came and gazed in
despair at the out-of-control men. Our volunteers and

staff were left shunting jumble up and down four floors without lifts (the union turned off the electricity). It was a shambles and left everyone very sad.

Despite our trades union problems, I set out to renew lost links with the Trades Union Congress of the United Kingdom. I took a television crew to see Len Murray and, with the crucial backing of Norman Willis (later the General Secretary himself), I held a party for the TUC in Mr Speaker's house. Speaker George Thomas felt that nobody would come (his modesty was legendary). He also said he had no alcohol (he is a Methodist) and that there was no budget, as his staff reminded me, too, for flowers. We plundered the Covent Garden market early that morning (an energetic volunteer gathered the ends of the traders' sales, telling them of our good cause) and Mr Speaker's House was filled with flowers for the evening. I took some crates of gin from my father, who was also willing to help, together with some Nicholson's whisky (distilled and bottled in Scotland under our family's name).

Contrary to George Thomas's expectations, all the TUC General Council accepted. I was given three minutes in which to outline the entirety of the Save The Children movement and ask for their help, as Norman Willis told me that was the standard maximum for TUC speeches. I managed it within my timescale and the Staff Association of the Inland Revenue came forward, took up our cause and ran an appeal. They were wonderful givers. Amusingly the handover of the cheque was a difficult time for me; never had I known donors who were so interested in the layout of our annual accounts!

The following year, Jumbly was held at Ally Pally (Alexandra Palace), a merry environment. Another 25,000 people came and so did Princess Anne. A splendid profit was declared by a satisfied Tim Phipps. The third year it was difficult to raise the same enthusiasm from the helpers. The Director General got whooping cough and chicken-pox (he thought it was jumble fleas and dust).

With strong displeasure, the volunteers carried a motion to stop the event.

Another idea was needed: I thought how about Slimathon? Lose a pound to save a child was the slogan. We ran that for three more years in *Woman's Own*. Next, the new editor, Iris Burton, and I ran an appeal for Westminster Children's Hospital. *Woman's Own* readers raised £1 million for the doctors and a whole new bone-marrow transplant unit was built in the hospital. It raised child recovery rates from twenty-five per cent to nearer seventy per cent because of the sterile environment and quicker through-put. Spending that money as the readers wished was a very difficult political battle in the NHS world, and the unit was later closed.

Keeping up with the swell of work overseas was a challenge. The suffering brought to light by our publications team, particularly when HRH The Princess Anne went on an overseas trip, was heart-rending and spurred us all on to greater fund-raising efforts.

1982 saw the birth of Stichting Redt de Kinderen, chaired by the then Chairman of Unilever, Frans van den Hoven, with as his Deputy Chairman a former Health Minister, Dr Kruisinga, and Secretary to the Board, Jan van Ommen. It was easier having a clean slate on which to work. With no contacts in the Netherlands there was freedom to choose just the right group. It took two years to convince the sober Dutch that this was something that they wished to do. On brief, bi-monthly visits I built up a stock of friends on which to draw. Unilever, Philips, the ABN (the Netherlands largest international bank), the Dutch Institute of Public Health, television networks, the Royal family; all seemed to offer sources of men and women of responsibility and influence who would understand the need to create this new charity. As the founder member I was on the Board for about eight years. The courteous Dutch held all their board meetings in English. My Dutch grew slowly but, even so, by the time I left to enter Parliament, I was still not proficient enough to be able to understand a board meeting in their own language.

Stichting Redt de Kinderen took up the Stop Polio campaign but with a difference, a truly fascinating one. Under the management of Dr Nicholas Ward, the classical polio vaccine was being used in southern Africa – three drops on a lump of sugar or, where no sugar was available, directly on the child's tongue. This is the live vaccine which takes the establishment of a full cold chain for it to reach the child and still be effective. The cold-chain system is expensive and difficult to run since the vaccine has to travel in the constant cold, and go into a freezer then into a fridge and finally travel in a cold bag in order to reach families right out in the far-flung villages of the African bush. Stichting Redt de Kinderen took an innovative approach and it was exciting and wonderful to be a part of this. We linked up with the Merieux Institute in Paris, which was developing an advanced version of the killed polio vaccine. It may be remembered that the early killed vaccine caused the polio deaths, and the disabilities that my schoolfriends suffered from.

The Merieux Institute for some time had been experimenting in further refinements which might create a safe, injectable killed vaccine. It was deemed that the time had come whereby the Merieux Institute and the Dutch Institute of Public Health could combine their work and use it in the field as a controlled trial under the guidance and watchful eyes of the WHO. We obtained permission from the Government of Burkina Faso (formerly Upper Volta). They were comfortable that their citizens would be used as a target group so that this new vaccine could be given a full trial.

Apart from the absence of the cold chain it has a number of other advantages: with an injectable vaccine the health worker can also incorporate other vaccines in the same visit to the child and thus provide several immunisations in one shot. The trials went ahead, the WHO agreed to supervise and screen, and the injections were remarkably effective. Steadily, Stichting Redt de Kinderen enlarged its work and moved to Benin next-door and then to other countries. Working with the Dutch was for me like coming home, in that they had this innate understanding both of the true duration of a project, and of the way medical research has a fundamental role to play in development.

Leaving the Save The Children Fund in 1985 was an enormous wrench. I missed particularly the past Chairman Dr Moynihan, who (with his wife Peg) had had much medical overseas experience before he rose to become Chairman of the Overseas Committee and then the Chairman of the Save The Children Fund. His great wisdom and merriment, his Irish sense of humour and frivolity took us through some dark moments indeed. Others I missed had already gone, and the new people with all their interests and excellences were coming in. I felt enormously privileged to play a part in the success of the Fund during my time with it, but its agenda had changed. It was time to move on.

6

Expectation and Action

The West has carried out so much good work in recent years in the developing world that expectations for help in difficulties are higher than they have ever been. But the gaps in culture and therefore understanding of different needs seem almost as wide as ever. Some overseas aid is so difficult to blend in with local culture that progress is almost impossible.

In the wake of the wars in Cambodia, Laos and Vietnam, refugees fled to Thailand. The camps on the Laos border were run by the United Nations. Impeccable in neatness they were large in terms of human misery. It looked as if the people there were going to be in camps for many years, perhaps for decades or more until they died. People came up with papers, begging for visas for the USA. In the baking heat a woman who had just completed labour was lying on an Indian-style bed with underneath her an open fire. This was supposed to burn away the afterbirth. Another woman, heavily pregnant and just going into labour, had a great rope tied round her middle, just beneath her breasts and above the fetus. This was the method used to stop the baby coming out of her mouth. There was a Western team of nurses from the UK trying to bring their standard mother/child health-care techniques into such unresponsive surroundings. It would be wrong to expect that the situation would be transformed overnight.

Some projects fail through civil war. One of the most poignant examples of this was during the fall of Vietnam. A film had been made which featured the senior Fund doctor in South Vietnam. It was impossible to forget his final words as he turned to the camera with the hordes of needy children around him, saying, 'I am not God.' Shortly after that, while swimming off duty, he drowned, and then, almost immediately, South Vietnam fell as an independent nation. The next pictures on television were those of aircraft leaving the aerodrome with mothers and children clinging to the doors and being pushed away. Then the American transporter crashed because it was overfilled with people. All voluntary efforts to help were nothing against the vast numbers of Vietnamese in need. Later still, there was the tragedy of the rejection of the boat refugees (the Boat People) by all countries save Hong Kong. The solution to these kind of problems lie with complex political negotiations – and we know how difficult they can be.

Sometimes the projects tried are much too involved. Some of the best ideas I heard of for southern Africans centred on tube wells, or special means of ploughing using normal tools (a wooden plough and an ox), or other such sane initiatives which can help people turn the corner in their own environments. Sometimes it is a case of simply developing the mechanisms they and their fathers have always used. The children's school-gardens initiative was in that category of usefulness. It is easy to teach a child how to grow vegetables and then how to cook them for their school lunch. The hope is that then the child will teach the mother if encouraged to do so. At the same time as looking at school gardens in southern Africa I heard of a great United Nations project: bringing in corrugated iron roofing for a massive new development, all in a heat rate of 40°C at midday. Imagine the effects of hot sun on all that metal. Clearly it was totally inappropriate to local conditions.

There is also the question of natural disasters. Robert

Rhodes James once made a speech in which he identified some African countries and the amounts of aid given to them since independence and contrasted that with the dramatic fall in their standards of living. Much later on, at a Royal African Society conference for the whole of Africa (their first for thirty years), I heard an explanation for this phenomenon from a senior geography professor. He was talking about the weather pattern of these same African countries and the decline in rainfall over the same period of time. Man against nature cannot be supported by overseas aid alone. Like it or not, we have to adapt to the changing face of our world.

There is the question of the correct choice of project, and the fact that too much money is as diversionary as too little. It gets spent uneconomically or on the less locally valuable projects. The German charitable world is a case in point. After the Dutch initiative I tried to form a French Save The Children Fund. I did not have quite the same response, which led me to do some research and to discover that in Catholic European countries almost all the aid is organised and spent effectively by the Church. It is the Protestant, or in the British case the Anglican, communities which do not give their Churches this vast responsibility. These countries tend to work in secular, as well as religious groupings and provide a multiplicity of options for fund-raising and project work. I moved on to try a Save The Children Fund in Germany but found an even more unusual situation. There are few charities in Germany because at birth each citizen is registered by their religion. And then a deduction is taken, as an Income Tax and given to each person's Church or sect, who then spend it on behalf of the citizens. That is why it is occasionally possible to see Lutheran pastors wandering round Africa with their pockets metaphorically bulging with national gold, urgently searching for suitable projects to support.

The satisfaction of raising £1 million very cheaply only

lasts if the expenditure is properly handled. Spenders in charities often belittle fund-raisers, but without money only modest action can be achieved. Transparently accountable expenditure reassures donors and funds-gatherers, and makes their job worth-while.

Achieving satisfaction for the spender is a matter of equal value. Here there were substantial differences in the Save The Children movement between the British and the Dutch patterns of work in the developing world. The British favoured a policy of replicability, whereby a project was carefully worked out so that it could be taken over locally and sustained, and then repeated a number of times. By this means, Western input for a project could be as little as three years. But did the work thus created last?

The Dutch looked at the terrain, saw how unpromising it was economically, socially and culturally and took a correctly pessimistic view of project handover. They allowed twenty-five years as a minimum for their first project in Burkina Faso (the old Upper Volta).

Their view seemed the more appropriate. Firstly, if a project is Western-created and responds to Western donor expectations then it will take a long while for non-Western staff to accept the conditions imposed from 'above' and to gain agreement to best tailor the project to genuine local requirements. Secondly, poverty does not disappear. If intervention from outside is helpful because of sparse local resources, for instance, then it is needed on a long-term basis. A swift project harms by raising hopes and unsettling local structures and conditions. Of course, the UK Save The Children Fund handles projects of many lengths, but the prevailing British culture was one of replication; the sound-bite term 'handover'. Maybe the Dutch were slow to form the new Netherlands Save The Children (Stichting Redt de Kinderen) because of their formidable thoroughness as a nation.

Sometimes aid ventures fail through man's inhumanity to man. The Health Minister in a South American country

(Colombia) pointed as imperiously as his Spanish fore-
bears to a map sprinkled with different-coloured circles.
'There you are,' he said, 'the blue are hospitals, the
red are health clinics and the green are village health
workers, all trained. We don't need any Western inter-
ference; our population is better cared for, health-wise,
than your own.' His complacency was clear. He did not
admit that not one of those buildings had been planned or
constructed. He just rejected the aid. The street children
were visible from his office window but he did not look out.
Nor did the Health Minister of another country (Mexico)
look out of his window at the crippled beggars below when
he marked the national polio-victim figures for the year as
zero. He wanted no vaccine, although the mothers did.

Sometimes a project fails through an inability to recognise the need for teaching fundamentals, such as
antenatal nutrition. More and more evidence shows the
effects on the brain of the child of malnourishment. In
one Central American country (Honduras) a nutritious
vegetable is traditionally spurned as worthless. The
mothers need that nourishment as there is an above-
average incidence of mental handicap.

Then comes the question of motivation, that most
difficult and least-questioned trigger of energy. In fund-
raising, economy of resources is a necessary goal. A
powerful Indian voluntary chairman of a national group
called Western aid-workers, 'Vultures of compassion'; a
phrase which stayed with me for ever after. She saw us
as predators who came to pick over the carcasses of the
poor and starving, pretending concern but really in the
business of satisfying ourselves. I have often thought of
her words when starving children come on the television
screen in Britain. Their pictures trigger a response and
then we turn away. Of course we know that once the cam-
eras have gone the suffering still continues. The difficulty
surely lies in deciding how to keep public concern high in
an appropriate way, not with a false compassion but with
a real concern and a determination to effect change. But

how to effect change from the outside without altering
the balance internally for the worse? That is the question
that we have to keep asking ourselves as we continue to
assist the poor and needy.

For some people, the disincentive for giving aid in any
shape or form is very large. 'Why help one child?' is a
question that is often posed. 'After all,' the speaker goes
on to say, 'there are hundreds of thousands like them
and if you can't help them all, there is little point in
helping any one of them.' That is the sort of person
who, if one particular child is not identified as needy,
then blusters past you with the comment, 'It's pointless
helping these millions of people, there are too many of
them and nothing will make any difference anyway.'
To respond aggressively is a mistake. For, with the
self-indulgence of a personal reaction, you are caught
on the eternal Morton's Fork (Henry VII's Chancellor's
two-pronged device) and the tormentor will neither help
the one child nor feed the five thousand. Surely, if you
cannot help many, you can at least do something for one
person?

Then there is the eternal difficulty of arguing on
cost comparisons. Western treatment for individuals is
very, very expensive and certainly in the context of the
developing world that same funding spent differently
could feed the veritable five thousand. Some people
say, 'Why spend all this money on one child?' If it is
possible to do, I think that there is no real choice. When
someone is suffering and you are given knowledge of their
suffering, I believe that you take on part of the burden
of personal responsibility for them as you are taken into
their confidence.

That's when your own personal strengths and weak-
nesses come into play, and that's where pulling out all
of the stops to work out the best programme of action for
the one person (or even the five thousand) becomes the
priority. It is critical not to allow a lack of clarity of vision
to inhibit you. Gathering new friends around you who will

share your perception of the suffering is crucial too. Then finding the time and ability to use their strengths and their different ways of helping is the next step. These are the building blocks of management everywhere.

The difficulties of starting up a charity are so much larger for the developing nations themselves. They have the disadvantage of being a unique and independent organisation patterned on Western models (Scouts, Guides, Boys Brigade) without much local wealth to tap for funds with which to chart their destinies. The task of teaching the developing nations methods of focusing their voluntary groups and ways of seeking funds internally and externally is a great challenge.

So what could I teach about building on the basics of practical action? Turning to the Duke of Edinburgh's Award Scheme was a change of task. Moving up an age group (dealing with mothers' and children's needs out of the Save The Children Fund is another world from handling teenage youngsters) was in itself a learning process. A whole unknown group of supporters with a completely different desire to help the young achieve their full potential gave me new challenges. We should be willing to try something new. In my case working closely with Prince Philip and Prince Edward offered a dimension of practical experience that I had not had before and they taught me much.

Take another instance. With the then Prime Minister of Turkey and his wife, I launched Turkey's first ever charity for women and children, the Daisy movement, in Ankara. I made my speech (in Turkish) to the whole Cabinet and the top 400 people in society. The charity started work by organising marriages for women whose children were outside the system and therefore gained no entry to education, health or any social care. The women had been deprived of marriage by the father's poverty or ill-will, since an unmarried woman was no burden financially on her partner. Marriages were organised for hundreds of women, and their children then became

accredited members of the society into which they had
been born. Others will have their own challenges but we
will always be willing to help and understand.

In Parliament, although I planned to leave aside the
voluntary world and bury myself in political challenges
in my constituency and also in London, to cut the link
has proved impossible. However, I have learnt something
else, that it is possible to define the areas of concern in
which to become involved in a voluntary capacity. With
so many good causes around, I have found it important to
be steadfast in turning away from the other enticements
on offer. Focusing on children, primary health care and
preventative medicine has given me a large link with my
earlier experience, while working for the handicapped
within the UK has provided a new and more public
challenge for me. The modern Parliament is the soft
target for all the pressure groups and it is difficult to
turn aside. But it is no use being a jack of all trades
and master of none. This is a temptation well worth
resisting.

Strangely enough, working in one specific area can
also help you to see political problems in a wider context. Chairing ADAPT (Access for Disabled People to
Arts Premises Today) has many difficulties and frustrations; for instance, we cannot hold meetings in the
House of Commons since it is ill adapted for people in
wheelchairs. However, this new responsibility gives large
opportunities for creating access for not only people with
disabilities, but also for those with the creaks and stresses
inevitably associated with the ageing process. And if you
look beyond that, why shouldn't a young mum with a
pushchair be able to bring her child easily into a picture
gallery or cinema? Somehow those questions have to be
addressed and they link into the parliamentary process,
with the potential for legislation on human rights for
those with disabilities. Impinging on that are semi-
monopolistic practices with the provision of equipment

for the physically disadvantaged. Moving on from there you enter the world of the mentally handicapped and the intangible problems of human rights for them. Chairing the Blind in Business gives opportunities to create information technology links for blind people in the workplace.

The House of Commons offers ceaseless opportunities for Members of Parliament to work on advancing human rights internationally. Inevitably, with my husband, Michael Caine, I find our shared concerns mesh with my public endeavour. Together we visited Auschwitz and Belsen on a private trip to Poland. There we grew to understand the advanced refinements of cruelty that one human being can practise upon another. Whether any of us are worshippers of God or not, surely such suffering of others raises profound questions about the substance of human nature.

In Belsen we saw the bunks built in the camp at the end of the railway line where several million victims were disgorged and housed like battery chickens in corrugated-iron hangars while awaiting execution in the concrete-ceilinged ultimate solution. I remembered there that the Hebrew word for hell in the Old Testament, Gehenna, is the word used for burning rubbish dumps outside the city walls. The word was apposite and accurate in redefining the places of extinction for the Jews. They were the rubbish of German society headed by Hitler, and as rubbish their lives were extinguished forcibly and their carcasses burned. The greatest refinement of cruelty, however, was in the design of the bunks on which they slept in their few nights before they entered hell. The cruelty of the designers was transparently apparent, the bunks were shaped so that the head was inches higher than the feet. The concrete rose just fractionally, presumably to remind the victims as they approached their death of the love and comfort once known to them as children when in their nursery bedrooms parents' hands had tucked soft pillows beneath their childish heads. Michael's and my hearts almost broke with sorrow, and the complete despair those victims must have felt reached out to us almost a half century on.

Keeping even such tragedies in the forefront of the public consciousness is difficult but internal knowledge remains secure for ever. Tragedies, however, are like Pelion upon Ossa. That is to say, one piles upon another and overlays the first until it is pushed out of sight. Different experiences, smells and sounds, new friendships with their stories of new tragedies pile in.

Michael and I were visiting Eastern Europe to try to understand the historic changes happening with the melting of the Cold War. Hungary, Poland and Czechoslovakia showed us the poverty of the people in the wake of failed ideology relentlessly imposed over the post-war period. In Poland, apart from the horrors of the concentration camps, we saw the love and dedication of work for crippled children and those with mental handicap, with nursing and teaching duties delicately discharged by unpaid professionals and volunteers.

The Polish children's charity, The Friends of Polish Children, had been known to me for many years. I had met their Chairman, an elderly paediatrician, Dr Serejski Jerez, at the Save The Children Conference where he, and a French speaker, could only communicate with me, as I had angered the American delegation by striking up a conversation with a Communist. The American position strengthened our bond and I have supported his work from afar for fifteen years. It was wonderful to find him still in his post in Warsaw and to be taken round by Dr Jerez himself, and by a senior professor at Warsaw University, with a Chair at Oxford, Dr Richard Hercinzski.

They took us to the hospital for handicapped children, where my small funding had purchased a few bricks for building. The hospital was like a Victorian one in Western Europe with long wards, iron bedsteads and few resources, but with a large amount of tender loving staff, overstretched and on slender salaries. The extent of handicap was acute. All sorts of children were there (many in their thirties, but with nowhere else to go) and some were grotesque, if visual criteria were applied. In the West, under the progressive legislation, most of these heavily deficient children would have been aborted. And in Poland also, the horrors of the general public to most severe handicap is such that the 'children' were kept in the hospital and only given parental and professional care. In recognition of my small funds raised, I was presented with a badge of honour as a patron of their cause.

On my return to Britain I tried to fund-raise for them, but the quality of care in Poland means that these children are not shown on our television sets and there were no sympathetic donations. It proved to be very, very difficult indeed to find a small sum of money or to interest anyone in assisting these half million parents and relations to continue a movement helping thousands of mentally and physically handicapped children.

Michael came with me also on a trip to Romania and Bulgaria at the request of Greville Janner, to look at religious prejudice in those countries. Greville had asked that at least one Christian MP came with the group to show that it was not an exclusively Jewish team. Knowing that I would be visiting Romania, I made arrangements to go to an orphanage, as I had seen the terrible pictures that had invaded Western living-rooms of Romanian babies and children tied by their arms and legs to cots. I knew I had to see what was really happening and guessed I had to help. The Austrian Save The Children Secretary General organised an invitation for me to visit a children's home in Bucharest. My colleagues asked to come as well when they learnt of my mission.

The home was vast, and 'home', as a word, was a misnomer. It was a grim institution housing 450 socially orphaned boys. That is to say their parents were still living but they had been dumped on the State at birth, with the abstraction by the parents of the funds supplied

by President Ceauçescu for each live birth, to assist the
enlargement of the Romanian population. Many of the
children come from gypsy stock and the Deputy Head
of the home proudly told me that he never touched
a gypsy child. It seemed to me that no one had ever
touched the children in kindness. Their shaven heads
were free of lice and they were unencumbered by any
possessions. Their iron beds were crammed beside each
other in barren dormitories. There was no hanging space
for clothes as they had none. They spent their lives, from
the age of seven to seventeen, there as the place was also
a school. Food was sparse and the cold was wicked, as
windows in the passages and rooms had broken glass and
the snow had piled in. The only hot water came once or
twice a day courtesy of the next-door factory when it ran
off steam.

On my return, and after Parliament had resumed
in October, I, with some other colleagues, set up an
All-Party Parliamentary Group for Romanian Children.
The Lord Chancellor and the Speaker were Patrons.
Colleagues such as Sir Geoffrey Pattie and Michael
Martin, Alan Beith and Ronnie Campbell, Tim Rathbone
and Arthur Bottomley all sprang to help. Over the next
twelve months, with the courteous assistance of Taylor
Woodrow, who loaned a Romanian-speaking engineer, we
rebuilt the orphanage and school. I started a Parliamentary Forum for all the Romanian children's charities in
the UK and discovered that 850 or more had been set
up. The larger charities declined to help as Romania had
too high a GNP for them to be involved. The small, new
groups carried out their remarkable work and all of them
had been started from scratch by people spurred on by
real and compelling compassion.

7

Evil in Iraq

I learnt of the Iraq atrocities in 1988 and responding to them has taken every ounce of my experience from previous work. Like the rest of the nation, I had watched in horror as the Kurds were sacrificed on the order of the brutality of Saddam Hussein. Those dreadful pictures – of chemically poisoned babies and children, dead on the ground, with their bodies inflated as if by pumps through the toxic material they had inhaled – had lived with me subsequently. The Gulf War followed in 1991. Like most of my Parliamentary colleagues I voted to save Kuwait. I also started immediately to look for ways of helping Iraqi victims. The war ended and the world acted to save the Kurds but not the Shi'ites.

I posed a supplementary in Foreign Office Questions in the House to Foreign Secretary Douglas Hurd. What were we going to do to help the war victims within Iraq after we had won? Would he consider some plans from myself for humanitarian aid? From the Government Front Bench, Minister Douglas Hogg responded immediately. Such plans would be welcomed. Could I please put them to him as soon as possible. I nodded agreement. He followed up his oral answer that day with a letter. Immediately, I approached the big oil companies to sound out their chairmen and chief executives. Would they be willing to help finance the building or rebuilding of a children's hospital in Baghdad? I knew that one would be needed fast; children are the worst hit victims and longest sufferers of any war. The companies were not interested. As I sought to create a spark between us, and to search out other possible donors for such a venture, the war ended, but not as I had hoped. Saddam Hussein remained in power and our enemy. The victims within Iraq were inaccessible.

The picture changed as swiftly again. In despair at his continuing rule, the Kurdish Iraqi population and the southerners (mainly Islamic Shi'ites) rebelled and fought (and lost) two wars internally. Thousands of the defeated fled. The southern victims left their cities under heavy military assaults by land and air and travelled in great pain and danger for days and weeks through the Iraqi marshes. They emerged unchecked by their new hosts, into south-west Iran. The Kurds tried to flee to Turkey, who allowed a number of refugees to enter and then closed the border.

The Western world reacted fast to try to save the Kurds, but took no comparable action for the Shi'ites. For myself, responding to their needs has taken every ounce of my experience from previous work, and that is wholly insufficient in the face of tragedy.

I knew nothing of the southern tragedy until I was invited to help with a Thames Television programme called *The Time, The Place*, which had sent a reporter to the Turkish mountains to interview refugees live by satellite, to link up on air with an audience in the London studio. A Labour Party spokesman would comment as a part of the audience response. Political balance required a Conservative speaker too.

In the same audience group as myself was the grandson of the Grand Ayatollah, Yousif Al-Khoei. He was making up the balance between Iraq north and south and, with his ninety-year-old grandfather trapped under house arrest in the south of Iraq, he knew the terrible consequences of the brave efforts his fellow countrymen had undertaken to bring peace and democracy to their country. Although he was not a politician Yousif had agreed to appear so that he could have a little time on the programme to talk about the horrors of the south as yet unknown to Western audiences. The producer had agreed, but on entering the studio he was told he could have just one sentence in the entire programme of an hour. 'One sentence for the suffering of my people?' he thought despairingly to himself, but took his seat none the less.

In the event, he was not even allowed that one sentence. Hearing my own concerns on the programme he came up to me afterwards and sought my help. In the wake of the programme I suggested to the audience that we hold a meeting in the House of Commons so that I could hear their story away from the television lights and sound. This was a Friday, and on the following Monday nearly 300 people came to the House of Commons, almost all Iraqi, both from the south and north. I offered nothing other than the forum and my ears, because to offer hope to people in terrible situations when you have not yet found something appropriate to give is something you should never do. It encourages a false optimism that rescue of some nature is on the horizon and we are back to the question of unrealistic expectations. If you cannot deliver that then you are guilty of diverting their scarce resources and energy to no purpose.

That meeting was followed by another one a week later and by another one a week after that. Then the meetings broke up in utter confusion, since people started to attend who were most clearly mouthpieces of Saddam Hussein. They stood up, bellowed and bawled and I had to call the police in to take them out. Naturally, the vulnerable people left immediately, melting like snow in the sun. I therefore began again with a very, very much smaller group of people who were clearly trustworthy, and worked with them. For the scale of terror, the enormity of the brutality and the ferocity of evil people inflicting pain on others was beyond any scale of comparison other than that of Hitler and the Nazis.

Dr Uloom, the wise and kindly London-based imam, took the community's role in briefing me. He told me terrible stories of tortures and executions, of medieval and barbaric treatment by Saddam's Republican Guard, of the sort we had come to know in the short time since Kuwait was liberated. John Simpson of the BBC triggered my resolve to visit the marshes. He asked me to debate briefly by satellite across the Atlantic on BBC's *Nine O'Clock News* with the Iraqi UN Ambassador. The Ambassador denied the stories of marshland genocide told to me by my friends. He asked me to visit Iraq and see, as a guest of the Government. His statements, magnified by the huge picture of him in the studio on a large screen, talking dismissively to me about repression, had to be investigated. I said that I would visit alone, and find out the truth. The die was cast.

I knew that I had to act. I raised money from private and Government sources for a small Iraqi charity under Dr Uloom's wing and became its patron. I first went to Iran in late August 1991 to help and came back in anguish, having found that the horrors I had anticipated were true. It was even worse than I had been told.

On the advice of my new Iraqi friends, I visited the Documental Centre for Human Rights in Iraq at its main office in Tehran to understand the sufferings of the Shi'ites more fully. I met with the Director, Thaìer Al-Haidary, and his organisation. A principal desire they held was that Western governments should recognise the Iraqi Opposition. They told me of the lack of knowledge of Western governments and their perceived weakness in failing to overthrow Saddam Hussein. They called on the West to give more attention to political problems and not to use the excuse of humanitarian aid to avoid these issues. They spoke of their desire for democracy in line with the citizens' wishes to elect their leaders. Was this not a fundamental right that most societies had? The

Iraqi people have been subjected to such oppression for a long time; should they not have this freedom too? They quoted the chemical attacks on their own people, not just at the time of the Kurdish massacre, but on a continuing basis. They said that Saddam Hussein would only give in to another threat of war.

They sought for world political assistance to overthrow the regime and give the citizens of Iraq power through democracy, and for external investment from the USA and Europe to rebuild their country. Could the West not use their economic power for the furtherance of democracy in Iraq? They thought that the Gulf War was not completed but merely suspended, and believed that it would be resumed until Saddam Hussein was defeated.

The quiet and simple rooms that the Documental Centre staff occupy contain such tales of horror and brutal torture that the weight of evil displayed near breaks the heart. Where have the modern Iraqi torturers learned their ghastly ways? From what source do they draw and maintain their mental force to continue to cause pain deliberately day after day, night upon night? What impels them to pick up a baby and smash its head to pulp against a door, to kill by beating with iron bars two small girls aged six and eight and then to stuff their bodies in a bin and seat the watching mother on top, then stand and jeer as her poor reason flees and she becomes insane? Is this the dark inheritance of the Ottoman Empire revisited on its victims' descendants? Or does such diabolical work spring fully armed like Pallas Athene from the head of Zeus?

The luckier Iraqi victims have found a safe haven by fleeing their homeland in secret with large difficulty into the safe haven of Iran. There they are given modest shelter, food and clothing in refugee camps run by the provincial governate in the southern province of Khozestaan. The refugee needs are also assisted by the Iraqi community in Tehran.

Near the Human Rights Centre the Iraqi Women's

Association found a home: in a small room, two floors up in a block of flats, about thirty women and girls work each day, putting together gifts of knitted or sewn items for families in the refugee camps, and, if they are lucky, making new abas (the black robe the Iraqi women wear). They talked of torture and oppression and begged for the moral backing of other women in the UK and elsewhere. In response to this call it strikes me that any woman's group either inside or outside the Church could make a link with this cause as a practical expression of solidarity.

Those torture or bomb victims who can be transported north find shelter in special hostels. I went to the home for the Iraqi wounded in Tehran, named inappropriately The Paris Hotel. The warmth of welcome of the superintendent, Ali Ja'afar Muhammed al-Wailee, to his patients and their visitors alike, transcends the simple surroundings in which he has to work and care for the wounded victims. The former hotel reaches four to five storeys upwards, with concrete stairways and small rooms leading off them, crammed with iron beds. Most of the men were too sick to move. One had his eyelids burnt off and most of the skin on his body by what was thought to be a napalm bomb. He was only a primary schoolteacher, with no political affiliations. Another's stomach hung out over his bed, strapped in from time to time by his visiting doctor, Dr Al-Hakim, a young and distant relative of the Ayatollah. Two more, suffering from kidney failure, were kept alive only by regular blood transfusions. They recalled the smell of the bomb that had pulled out their insides through their mouths and bowels as resembing garlic. That meant it was a chemical weapon, internationally an illegal method of attack on armed forces and still less upon defenceless civilians. Still another sought frantically to go to the West for surgery that could never repair his spine; he was yellow of face and trapped for ever in a wheelchair, paralysed from the neck downwards. His hands and arms were strapped to the arms of the wheelchair by bandages to help him keep a seated position and not slump down. He had been buried underground for four years with many others, and beaten so viciously by the guards towards the end of his imprisonment that he will never move again. Somewhere in his mind is the belief that Western surgery will bring back his mobility. Another victim has lost most of his bottom jaw.

The beautiful girl brought in for a consultation, with her profile faultless from the side view, turned towards the light and showed the socket where her other eye was destroyed by a bullet. Her father was in despair since his daughter could never get married now, as who would want a deformed wife? The Koran places physical beauty in women, particularly, as of high importance. Indeed, the old Arabic saying tells that: 'The beauty of a woman is in her face, the beauty of a man is in his mind.'

The young man with his left leg bandaged and bent from foot to hip pleaded ceaselessly for an operation. Yet, when the surgery was offered he refused, since it involved amputation below the knee. It was hard to convince him that gangrene would eventually kill him.

From Tehran it is possible to fly south, over many hundreds of miles of sugar-cane, farmlands, pale desert and high snowy mountains. Behind the city of Isfahan the Iranian Red Crescent had erected a camp for 2,000 Iraqi refugees. The term the Iranians use for the refugees, 'our uninvited guests', displays most accurately their extraordinary hospitality to those in need from other nations. Iran now gives refuge to some 3.5 million people who have fled from their own internal troubles. The Indian population from Kuwait, destitute thousands from Afghanistan and Iraq give the Iranian Red Crescent the largest national workload of any Red Cross/Crescent member organisation. Iran has her own displaced people too. The aftermath of the Iran–Iraq War is still felt by those Iranian citizens whose towns were destroyed by Scud missiles and farmlands drenched with chemical weapons. In southern Khozestaan some of the camp dwellings inhabited by the Iraqi refugees were hastily erected as temporary homes for local homeless families in the mid-eighties.

I visited a new camp in central Iran, run by the Red Crescent. Isfahan city contains the most beautiful mosque in the world, covered with mosaics of turquoise, silver and gold fashioned into Persian flower-like pattern trellises on fluted columns. The domes shine and sparkle in the sun. The architect practised on the Taj Mahal before he created his masterpiece here. Outside the provincial capital and at the foot of a high mountain range stretched lines of tents, the temporary shelter for 2,000 Iraqi refugees. The thoughtful and efficient Red Crescent co-ordinator worked hard on the logistics of food supplies and sanitation, medical clinics and hospital care. He showed me the books and took me around the camp. It was impressive work carried out in stark circumstances. The wind off the mountains was so powerful that it whipped sand through the tents, shredding the canvas. The tents were replaced every two months by the Iranian Army because of this.

Further south, his colleague, Mr Moghaddam in Khozestaan province, showed me how his organisation cares for in total perhaps some 50,000 refugees, most of whom were from the cities, towns and villages of southern Iraq. They told me tales of summary evictions, deaths and dark horrors. Their great yearning was to return home, but many of their homes had been destroyed and over the camps hung a pall of near tangible despair. This was the new Palestine in the making. Without a miracle, those able and intelligent people would be there for the rest of their lives. No appropriate education was available for their Arabic-speaking children in Farsi-speaking Iran. Although both peoples share the Shi'ite Muslim faith their history and non-religious culture differs as much as that of France and England. The two national identities seemed to me to be as strong and distinctive as those of

China and Japan or Spain and Portugal. Job possibilities failed the linguistic barrier too, and the men told me they were mostly confined to the camps since they could not find productive work outside. Retaining family values was already placing large strains on the mothers when their offspring had no outlet for their energies and enthusiasms and fathers were often dead or missing. Tragic tales were commonplace. One woman gave me her story for almost the first time she had spoken at all to anyone since it had happened. Her husband was among hundreds herded into a line and run down by a file of tanks driven by jeeringly triumphant Iraqi soldiers. Her speech was faltering, her eyes filled up with tears.

In the camps the refugee doctors showed me the simple clinics with which they tried to provide medical care. The refugee teachers showed how difficult it was to teach without books. The refugee spiritual leaders were offering care and the love and knowledge of God in circumstances that spoke primarily of man's inhumanity to man, and also as hurtfully of the determined ability of others in more comfortable and secure surroundings in other countries to just forget their sufferings.

Away from the camps and huddled in primitive shelters around the neighbouring towns of Ahwāz and Shūshtar I found a further group of refugees, numbering about 5,000. They had fled to Iran before the camps were set up in March 1991. Their plight was even worse than that of the refugees. I travelled further along the borders, a few hours' drive away, and met with some families from a group of 10,000 people, who wander like ghost families mourning their loss of homes and livelihoods. Deep in the marshes, behind the battle lines and thus beyond my vision, I heard of half a million more. They could not reach the safety of Iran, or they could not bear to leave their homeland, and continued to risk destruction there. I knew that I must try to visit them.

For my trip to the marshes I took with me the ITN crew from Belfast, Trevor Yates (cameraman) and Andrew

Simmons (reporter). Our translator was Dr Haydar
Hassan, the heavily tortured victim of the Saddam
Hussein regime who had escaped during the Gulf War
due to the Allied bombing of the prison in which he
was confined, the Al Ghraib prison in Baghdad, where
political prisoners, many of them Shiah, are detained
and executed. He had reported that twenty to thirty
executions are still taking place daily, along with a great
deal of torture (three other doctors had also confirmed this
to me). With us was Hazemi Al-Haidary, the Public
Relations Officer in the office of Ayatollah Al-Hakim. He
had lived for some time in the marshes before he escaped
to Tehran.

We sailed in a small boat with a diesel-fuelled propeller
engine. We took two cans of diesel oil, some food and
bottled water with us. The boatman, who was called
Ashor, was assisted by his brothers. Like our guide,
Mohamed, he was a marsh Arab whose family had
lived inside the marshes for ever. The brothers, Ashor,
Mohamed and Ali, just gave me these shortened versions
of their names. Like everyone else they were fearful of
repercussions on their families if captured or if I revealed
their true identities. A young mujahedin, a volunteer
Iraqi fighter against the regime, sat beside me in the
boat holding a rusty Russian repeater rifle. Spent bullets
dropped back into the boat and lay in pools of water.

We sailed swiftly into the marshes, up wide waterways
which were bordered by towering banks of grey and
green reeds of the thickness of a hazel wood, but much
more dense. It was not possible to see through them
except for the occasional gap when we caught glimpses
of other narrow winding waterways. The only noise was
that of distant firing, the continuing crackle of bullets.
Our engine disturbed the peace and seemed very loud
indeed.

About an hour inside, we came across a series of barriers designed as traps to stop our progress. These were of
military hardware. Tanks were positioned in the centre of

the waterway, strung with barbed wire from side to side. Chunks of concrete, rusted big guns and iron poles used as boomerangs, together these gave an obstacle course which made movement further into the marshes difficult and slow. We progressed very cautiously, ducking under the thin wire and zig-zagging round the tanks and other hardware. Our guide told us that the blockade had been put up by the Iraqi Army to prevent refugees escaping from the marshes to Iran where they would be safe. When the refugees reached the blockade their progress was slowed down so much that the Army could catch them up and shoot them down.

After another two hours we had gone through the obstacles and, on turning a corner, were shot at unexpectedly by a rifle glinting out of the banks of tall reeds on the far side of a small lagoon. Our guard shouted repeatedly that we were friends and after another two rounds of shots we persuaded the fighter that we were on his side and he put down his weapon. We sailed on further and found a group of people who had assembled to meet us and whom the fighter had been guarding. They were all hungry and told us they had not eaten for three days. They were not normally together but braved the dangers of betrayal by informers in order to brief us on the sufferings of their people. We gave them the food we had in our boat. They ate a part of it immediately and saved part for their companions hidden further inside the marshes. One of them, known as Nishim, gave me a present of the only thing he had, a gilded pen. His only other possession was a grey Army blanket. Each of them had one blanket or piece of clothing in which they slept and then just the clothes they stood in. They had no shelter, only the single blanket; the water on which we sailed to drink; and lived hand-to-mouth for food, depending on isolated boat routes and supplies which managed to get through to them.

Nishim told me the story of the women and children they had left behind. He offered to take me into the area of Saddam's Army, a five-day journey by road, which had to be undertaken at night. I discussed it with Trevor and Andrew and they said since they could not film there was no purpose in their going. I was much tempted, but decided to stay with the film crew as our purpose was to get the pictures and story to the world and not to have unnecessary adventures. I promised Mihsin I would come back and go there with him another time.

Each of the men bore scars from sadistic torture or war injuries. One had a badly twisted arm, which I found to be a common injury, caused by prolonged hanging from the ceiling for hours, days and weeks. The blood supply is cut off and the bones begin to twist irreversibly into an unnatural shape. A doctor I met subsequently showed me proudly how he had saved his right hand for surgical work in the days of freedom by balancing his weight on his left arm when hung from the ceiling by his captors each day. His left hand and arm were grossly misformed but his right hand was unharmed.

Our friends told us of a vast battle which had taken place ten days before on 20 September 1991, when a heavy contingent of the Iraqi Army, the Republican Guards, had surrounded a city named Mainmona and its surrounding villages of Al Shudairia, Abokobra, Altala, Alaithah and Al-gzaiza, together with Alsalam city. They had torn up the roads from these cities and villages and then applied a total siege. In the area they had arrested many people in their homes. This had followed on from another attack some days earlier on the Sheik Saiad city where the same siege conditions had been created. They told us also of the way in which the Guards had taken lists of names of the people who had taken part in the uprising and who were the first targets for arrests and executions.

We sailed on for another two hours and found ourselves suddenly in a huge area of clear water. A shot rang out and we could see a reed hut in the left-hand corner of the marsh border and to the right a man guarding that little camp with a rifle trained on us. In the middle of the lake I saw there were more men in another boat with all their guns on us. They also shot at us and Trevor, grumbling, said, 'I think my hand shook then.' There was a great deal of shouting across the water and our guide persuaded them we were friends as we came towards them. We photographed them shooting at us as we came. At the reed house, with the guns still on us, I went inside and sat down with two freedom fighters. They were twenty-two and twenty-three years old and had been involved in the uprising. They were marked men who had left their mothers, sisters, wives and children to fight against the oppressor. They told me that the marshes and villages were completely surrounded by the Army, with no food because the women could not get out to get it. Both young men were scratching away at the bites on their bodies from the mosquitoes which were all around us. This is a malarial area.

We left them and went on to the next lagoon, through an overgrowth of reeds, and the motor of our engine stopped many times on the encroaching vegetation. People got out of the boat and pulled and pushed, and pulled and pushed. I found my black lace head-dress and long blue robe (the marsh Arab women's dress) a welcome barrier against the hard blows of the papyrus branches as they sprang back and the continuing nuisance of the malarial mosquitoes. Eventually, after many such stoppages, we reached another wide water lagoon with signs of burning and scarring, a gigantic bomb crater with scorch marks many meters long, and Army debris. We could see smoke rising less than a mile off and were told that Saddam Hussein's men were burning marsh reeds in an effort to smoke out people in hiding. The evidence of burning which we had seen we were told had been caused four weeks earlier by the Army, which had been sent to smoke out the Shi'ites hiding there.

It was getting dark and we saw some people on a reed island and went to join them through more warning shots. Our friends there built a fire and started to cook bread with a little old flour and marsh water. There was no oven; the paste was patted into a circle and pushed under the hot ashes of the reed fire bed. It came out blackened with the inside still raw. Someone there said that he had seen many people flee through to the marshes – a hundred or more just in the last two weeks. Some had come from another village nearby that the Army had assaulted a few days earlier in the very marshes where we were standing. Other ways to leave were to go to the cities and stay with relatives before simply disappearing to try to travel over the borders from the north. The villages were very unsafe and Saddam Hussein's informers were now in them. The places which had once been easy to hide in were now under siege. Most of the people I saw in the marshes were armed with small rifles.

Six weeks earlier there had been reports of a price of 10,000 dinars to be paid for those in hiding on production of their heads to Saddam Hussein in Baghdad. This was a worrying new dimension. A former farmer added that the personal danger even to those who had not rebelled against Saddam Hussein had become so great that it was necessary for him to leave. He had farmed north of Basra, but the attacks were now carried out with such frequency against the villages in his area – using bombing, ground attack, tanks, fixed-wing aircraft, helicopters mounted with sub-machine-guns – that the people were forced to flee. Men speaking through loud-hailers from helicopters had threatened to use chemical weapons on those who remained. People had fled to the marshes to escape. I asked the farmer how large a typical village was. He said that each village had about seventy to eighty houses, with each house being the home of a family of perhaps ten people. When villages were emptied of their inhabitants the houses were occupied by the Army to keep the villagers from returning. Many were killed during the attacks and many were just arrested and not seen again. One victim of bombing said he had seen forty-three people executed by a tank running them down.

None of these men had any shelter other than the reed huts we saw. They slept in a different place each night to avoid detection, and lived alone. Another man, middle-aged, said that he had just seen ten days of heavy fighting in Al Karam and that fighting was still going on in some of the areas where he had been twelve days before. He had also seen the heavy shelling of Mosa, Amhush and Maiar, on 9 September 1991, by nine helicopters with heavy guns on board. He estimated that about 400 Iraqi soldiers had been involved in the campaigns against these villages. He went on to name a number of the women and children who had been killed in Amhush and Mosa.

It was now totally dark and it seemed right to move on. Our presence anywhere only added to the possibilities of discovery of the marsh people by the Army. We re-entered the boat and tried to go back to our starting point. Our boatmen were becoming concerned that we were too close to the front line of Saddam Hussein's Army and we must go back and exit the marshes as fast as possible. I knew that by our presence we were bringing potential dangers on the people we were visiting. Our exit journey proved to be extremely difficult. Our guide suddenly became very sick and vomited for an hour over the edge of the boat. He was the only person who knew the way. He had been born and bred in the marshes and knew every branch of the waters in the part of the marshes we were in. Even the boatman's brothers did not know the way out. However, they were determined to try and, despite Trevor's suggestion that we remained where we were, we travelled on and on in the dark. Sometimes, as protection against attacks from hiding refugees, our guards fired shots in the air. We went in and out of water alleyways and skirted around lagoons, diving back in again in a different direction. We were lost and had run out of bottled water and food and there was little fuel left. I settled down in the boat and nodded off to sleep briefly as I had no bump of locality which would assist.

As suddenly as he had become ill, the guide, grey with

vomiting, recovered. His eyes returned to normal and he said with great concern that we were a mile from the front line and must retreat at once. Hours later, we ran out of diesel fuel, but by that time we were close enough for another boatman to come from base and refuel us. We contacted him by mobile telephone, which due to working only within a twenty-mile radius had until then been of no value to us further inside the marshes. I believed that it would be possible for me to go inside again, and so it has proved.

On my first visit to Iran I quailed mentally in the face of the immensity of suffering. I felt weighed in the balance and found wanting. The widow's mite would need multiplying a million times to effect a cure for evil on this scale. But if a start were not made, however small a one, nothing could be achieved. And, since no human condition remains constant, without beneficial change the situation would deteriorate still more. I recalled that the obliteration of the Jews by Hitler was worsened by the liberal West's delicate eyesight; by the determined blindness of those who could really see, just as the refugee Palestinians' continuing despair should stir us to act. For outsiders to turn aside because a human problem offers no easy answer is surely the mark of cowardice, to me, the mark of Cain. But how to help the Iraqi victims? That was the task. The food, clothing and other goods now being purchased for the refugees from the money given to me by the British Government would be most welcome, but far more was needed and for the borders and marshes too. Both places were inaccessible and dangerous. The only answer was to take the long view and to begin to walk with the victims and beside their quiet, Iranian hosts.

Among the victims was Amar.

8

A Boy Called Amar

Amar, who has given my husband and I so much pride and happiness, came into our lives in an unexpected way. As he himself said to Michael, now his adopted father, recently: 'Isn't it funny, Emma came to see me in Iran and asked if she could help me. I said she could, and here I am.' I remember it most clearly. Travelling from the camps into the marshes of Iraq on my second visit in late September 1991, I stopped at the border town of Ahwaz to meet some victims of Saddam Hussein. Down a side street, with closed doors in tall mud-brick walls lay a house euphemistically called 'The Home For The Wounded'. I had asked if a number of particularly badly wounded people could be available to meet me and to give me their stories in front of a camera. Why so? Because on my first trip to the area a few weeks earlier, I had painstakingly recorded some of the most terrible stories that had ever been told to me directly, by victims whose families had been demolished, towns burnt to the ground and lives destroyed some months earlier when the south of Iraq, together with the Kurds in the north, rose up to try to topple the tyrant, Saddam. They had failed and his vengeance had been terrible. On my return to Britain I tried to tell their stories, but was told quite simply that the victims were exaggerating.

It was the very stillness of Amar's despair that entered my heart. His utter stillness, seated on a wooden slatted

bench inside the door as I stepped through from the
street. It was terrible to behold. His face and body had
melted in the heat of flames from aerial bombardment
of the grain silo to which his family and neighbours had
fled as Saddam's planes flew overhead. The pilots saw the
fleeing people, targeted the silo in which they had taken
refuge and dropped their napalm and phosphorus bombs
directly on that shelter. Nearly all of the 300 people
inside had died, burned alive, but Amar had escaped
and run, burning with flames but covering his eyes,
towards the river he knew so well nearby. Just past
his ninth birthday, his speed and quick-witted action
saved his life initially. He dived in, and eventually the
burning ceased. Then, lifted by kindly soldiers into a
truck driven by the Opposition he, along with other
older wounded men, got into the marshes and after a
lengthy and dangerous journey came into the safe haven
of south-west Iran.

There, in a small local hospital, Iranian surgeons managed to save his life, with patchwork-quilt but careful
surgery. They took skin off his legs and back to keep
his face in being and after three months of which he
could remember nothing, mercifully, he was discharged,
an orphan. The Home For The Wounded took him in
and there I found him, scarred and still bleeding from
the surgery and his injuries, in dreadful unceasing pain.
He was existing in a three-storey, simple house where
every room was packed with iron bedsteads and young
and bitter men. For they were wounded, too, their world
destroyed, and all their efforts to make a better Iraq and
free themselves and their families from the tyranny of
Baghdad had come to nought. There, every day was
spent in bitter and angry discourse. It was no place
for a child. Not that Amar looked like a child; his
injuries had made him old. The bomb had dropped
upon him when he had just turned nine years old,
but this motionless, pain-filled, bleeding and rigid boy
was ageless in his despair and agony. He was away

from us on a plane of suffering that was outside our comprehension.

The wonderful good fortune was that with me I had two extraordinary people, and another one awaited me in the Home For The Wounded. Vahid Farmand, First Secretary in the Persian Gulf Department of the Iranian Foreign Ministry had three of the most beautiful small daughters I had ever seen. I had met them on my first trip, weeks before, when with his wife we became close friends. Also standing beside me was someone who had been a victim of torture himself – a plastic surgeon, Dr Haydar Hassan. This was not his real name, but with a brother still locked up in Baghdad's prison, for over eleven years, unheard of by his family, he dared not risk exposing him in case he was alive, so he dropped the family name. And, standing a little way away from Amar, was the man who had made this meeting possible, Abu Hydar al Moduss, from the Documental Centre for Human Rights based in a dusty room in Tehran. It had been to him that my Tehran-based friends had turned just at the time when – in despair at the inadequate and negative response I was receiving in the West when speaking of the Iraqi Shi'ites and their plight – I had asked to meet some of the worst victims in person. The idea was to film and record their sufferings for a world-wide audience.

I could see no other way for Amar than seeking Western medical treatment. This meant finding money, surgeons and a hospital, paperwork (passport and visas) and a home for him. It was a huge task. But it had to be done. Amar's face and bearing, his despair and gallantry had touched me profoundly. His plight lay in the back of my mind during our long hours inside the marshes. After we had got out I asked to see him once more. I suggested a plan to the others and we all swung into action. Our aim was to get Amar to the United Kingdom for crucial surgery, and to return him to a loving family (to be identified) in Iran for him to grow up safely and out of pain. Maybe the situation in Iraq would subsequently alter for the better and he and the unknown family could then return. We knew that his own family were dead; he was an orphan from the storm.

And so the Amar Appeal was born. The initial intent was to help Amar himself and, once that was in hand, to help as many others like him to start their lives again, with the provision of surgery, medicines, food and clothing. The Iranians' generosity was stretched to breaking point by the volume of refugees and the acute needs they brought with them. I felt profoundly that we in the West were allowing Iran to carry this vast burden of suffering alone. We had to help.

Back in the United Kingdom I sought a six-month visitor's visa for Amar for crucial surgery. Colleagues in Tehran found immediate sympathy and understanding for Amar's plight from Chargé D'Affaires David Reddaway in the British Embassy (the gateway to the UK). Finding the funding meant triggering a public appeal, and on no money.

I sought the help of the only group who could make that happen within the time-scale: the media. Newspaper men who really merited that age-old term, hard-boiled, softened on seeing Amar's photographs. The two-man ITN team with me had used their skills. Sharp-witted George Parker of the *Western Morning News* witnessed all kinds of actions by this particular West Country MP. His editor ran the appeal and West Country readers took up the challenge. The *Today* newspaper picked it up and gave it a brief push.

On my return from the marshes, I had also sought out the United Nations. I learned of the appointment of a former UN Commissioner as the Special Rapporteur for Human Rights in Iraq, Prince Sadruddin Aga Khan, and went to meet him in Geneva in late October 1991. I gave him a full report of the atrocities I had witnessed. He took my independent report to Baghdad in December 1991 to show to Saddam Hussein, first-hand evidence of the genocide he had been denying. Saddam Hussein still did not admit to it and claimed that the British MP had fabricated her report. Sadruddin Aga Khan then resigned, saying that negotiation with Saddam Hussein was not a possibility.

In despair I turned to the forum of the House of Commons and requested a Consolidated Fund debate from Mr Speaker. He granted it. I rose to my feet early in the morning just before Christmas to speak to an empty Chamber save for the Minister, Mark Lennox-Boyd, and myself. The Minister for the next debate, John Maple, walked in to give his moral backing. Someone was on the Opposition benches, as they always are. But in the Chair was Mr Speaker, Bernard Weatherill, and it was to him that I told the story about Amar. A quarter of the way through I saw tears upon his face. He left the chamber hastily on completion of the debate at six a.m. went to his desk and wrote me a note saying: 'You have reduced me to tears, something that no one has ever done in the Chamber before. This is for the poor child whom you have told me about this morning when I was in the Chair.'

The fund-raising breakthrough came when Ivan Fallon of *The Sunday Times* agreed – on seeing the ITN video which I took to show him together with the *Hansard* of the debate – to run a full-scale appeal to raise the funds to bring Amar to Britain. That was a wonderful thing since all the fund-raising that had been achieved by then was wholly insufficient to face the costs of real, extensive plastic surgery for this one special boy. *The Sunday Times* back page carried Amar's face and readers responded with great generosity through thousands of modest personal donations. It reminded me of how people can care about an individual, it is the weight of mass suffering that causes even the most thoughtful of people to feel so inadequate that they do nothing to abate it.

Those with professional skills do not respond with that pessimism if it is possible to offer them a way of using their skills to help. The medical profession was a case in point: Vahid Farmand's photograph of Amar in *The Sunday Times* brought offers of help from plastic surgeons in Denmark, the USA and Britain. Sir Philip Harris, an old and close friend, strongly recommended Guy's Hospital, of which he was the Chairman. Independently, Guy's senior plastic surgeon, Anthony Rowsell, made contact. I knew that we would be secure in that great London hospital and Tony's calm personal and professional optimism created an immediate bond. The pieces of the puzzle Amar had posed me were starting to come together. I learned that he had been given a passport and a visa too.

However, there was continuing hostility from some of my constituents, who objected strenuously that their Member of Parliament should bother with 'those foreigners'. Many people in the West just did not seem to care that, far away and out of sight of the occasional television camera, ferocious murders, torture, rapes and mass burials of victims were taking place. As for Iraq, it was enough for them that some people were contributing to Kurdistan. The Simple Truth Red Cross Appeal was under way, the West felt that they had 'done Iraq' and that should be enough.

I returned to Geneva a second time in February 1992, to speak to the UN Committee for Victims of Torture, with Amar who came there from Tehran to meet me, for the entry into the United Kingdom. Together we made a presentation to the United Nations. This was made possible by courtesy of a small French woman, a left-wing professor of politics, heading a human rights organisation out of Marseilles. No one else would give us space, even the British Save The Children Fund, who turned down three requests from both myself and from the British Mission in Geneva. So it was left to a French woman from the opposite side of the political divide to give me two minutes of her crucial slot that she had waited for for a full twelve months for her own cause. (The British Mission persuaded the Chairman from cutting off the

microphones when we overran our time.) She spoke so
fast in her eight minutes that the translators could not
understand and ran forward to try to get her to slow down.
She did not break her speed. I then came on, with Amar
standing stiffly by my side. I spoke so fast that the official
Iraqi delegation could not understand me, they only heard
the word Iraq and came up afterwards to thank me so
much for talking about their country. I told them they
were despicable and that I was against them. They, and
their regime, were responsible for the damaged boy who
stood beside me.

So Amar came home, to the United Kingdom. Now we
are twelve operations further forward and he is a child
again. His first football boots, his prized black jeans, his
neat but scorned school uniform and bedroom drawer full
of computer games, give us large pleasure as the proofs
of change and happiness. Michael's daughter, consultant
clinical psychologist, Amanda Caine, has always said that
no individual characteristics, beliefs and behaviour are
unalterable. Amar, by means of his determination and
with the help of others from different professions, is
proving her right each day. The Iraqi community in
London – his constant visitors in hospital – has faded
from his mind. Now he is in an English community
college and works so hard at languages, including French,
plus science, physical education (the easy one) and other
subjects. His personal teacher, Dr T. Hashim, came
to us through the introduction of Dr David Harrison,
Vice-Chancellor of Exeter University and past Chairman
of the Vice-Chancellors' Committee. Homework is coming
out all right and, to Amar's own surprise, he was elected
form captain by his new classmates on his second term.
His astonishment at this was so profound that he did not
tell us for at least two weeks, lest it should melt away.
He is a continuing surprise and joy.

An unexpected helper in the world of Amar's pain and
treatment is the superstar Michael Jackson. His singing

and his dancing are enjoyed by children and many adults, and that he has chosen voluntarily to undergo plastic surgery helps us now, so much. Every parent will recognise the value of the many posters decorating Amar's bedroom of Michael Jackson, arm strapped in plaster cast and fingers in Band Aid. This is of great help (or so Amar thought when he broke his arm recently). But Michael Jackson has also chosen to undergo surgery to reshape his face and this is fundamental to our family's success in going through Amar's operations in the past and those ahead in the future.

Guy's Hospital gave us a semi-permanent room for months in the Rothschild Ward high on the tenth floor of their modern tower block with its historic views over Southwark Bridge in London. That is the ward where children often hover between life and death and where critical heart surgery is regularly performed. Life-support machines placed beside televisions with video and computer games are normality here. Playgroup leaders mix with teachers in the simple classroom at the far end of the passage. Nurses and sisters go about their duties with alertness and diplomacy and this framework has created a background of firm support.

Soon after his arrival in hospital, Amar became a Ward of Court with myself having care and control, and the official solicitor entered our lives in the form of the elegant Veronica Carter. A swell of Iraqi friendship surrounded Amar on his entry into Britain. A place was offered to him at a first-class Iraqi school and unselfish and suitable Iraqi families offered their homes in London. But Amar has made his choice. He is in England and he wants to learn English, attend an English school and live with an English family in a village in Devon. And that is what he is doing.

Sometimes I find Amar with tears down his cheeks in sleep. The nightmare image that he has found so difficult to shift himself is that of an old man run down in front of his eyes by a tank. For night upon night, and through the

day as well, the old man's face as he was crushed beneath
the earth, with that of the soldier driving the tank jeering
above him as he carried out the murder has lived with
Amar. Little by little it has started to fade but it will be
difficult to lose for all of his life.

The story of Amar's progress since he settled in and of
those who are supporting him so unselfishly belongs to
another book. The sufferings of those left behind have
worsened.

9

Long Memories, Short Memories

Victims of torture find it hard to talk about their suffering
with those who have not experienced it too. On another
trip to Iran, with money from the EC for food and clothing
for the refugees, in February 1992, Iraqi Shi'ite spiritual
leaders gave me a greater understanding with new and
terrible knowledge brought from the marshes.

The headquarters of the spiritual leadership of the
Iraqi Shi'ites in Iran is a plain building in Tehran. Here
Ayatollah Al-Hakim has simple offices. His room is lined
with photographs of his family, young and middle-aged
brothers, uncles and cousins. All are now dead, executed
or kidnapped and tortured to death by the Baghdad
regime.

In 1981 Ayatollah Al-Hakim was captured in Baghdad
and put in an underground cell in which the previous
occupant had gone completely mad. The cell was deep
in the earth and the darkness was complete. For three
months he lived in it, taken out only to be tortured and
then thrown back and locked up again in the complete
blackness. His tortures were extreme. He held on, praying
all the time. In the end his torturers declared that he must
have that condition that some people had which meant
that their flesh felt nothing, they had no sensation. How
else could it be that he uttered no sound throughout the
most extreme of pains inflicted on him by themselves?
They stopped, concluding it was pointless.

He told me all this in Tehran nine years later at three o'clock in the morning. At the end of a meeting he looked into the middle distance and said reflectively, almost apologetically, how difficult it was *not* to recall that pain. In response to my only question, he replied that he had never felt so close to God.

He recounted some of the methods used to hurt him. It all came out and suddenly, after about twenty minutes, he shook himself and said, 'But I must not go on like this. Many people have suffered so much worse than me. In any case,' turning to the other person in the room, Sheik Hahmoodi, 'he has suffered more than me. We all have, let him speak now.' A similar tale of horror, talked about in the most normal of voices came from Sheik Hamoodi.

He had been arrested one morning in late April 1975, while he was starting his journey to sit the final examination for a post-graduate degree. A security agent had stopped him at a road junction only a few yards from home. He was taken to the primary security detention centre of the Baghdad area, known as a place where people are interrogated and tortured. There, a squad of ten security men led him back home, where they searched all his belongings. They paid special attention to any book that referred in any way to Shiahs or Shiism, even if the author of the book had died over a thousand years ago. His mother, who at the time was in her seventies, watched all this with bewilderment. She bade him farewell unable to conceal her tears. He believed that she was silently praying for his safe return.

On his return to prison he was immediately tortured. This was accompanied by questions about other people and his links with them. After each question, the beatings became harder and more savage. They tied his hands behind his back, secured them up on a ceiling fan, and kept striking and punching him until he became unconscious. Every time he screamed, they would put their shoes and feet on his mouth. Frequently, they ordered him to run and hit him while he was moving. Their language was vile, with obscene, religious abuse. He was then locked into an isolated cell with a rudimentary toilet, which was filthy and odorous.

In the compound there were so many detainees that physical movement was impossible for any prisoner. Sleep was only achieved in a seated position and always there would be someone nearby who had just had his nails pulled out, or a person agonising after a savage beating. Alternatively, one of the detainees would be screaming all night, because of the torture. There was little food. The prison wardens periodically took out a small group of detainees, and practised on them any torturous rituals that they fancied, just to display their power. As a result of all this, some prisoners committed suicide. Two weeks of this agony ended with Sheik Hamoodi's transfer to a larger detention centre called 'Al-Fudhaliah', located on the eastern edge of Baghdad, an area that was mainly agricultural and well known for buffalo farming. This detention centre was previously a stable for animals belonging to the royal family prior to the downfall of the monarchy in July 1958. During the so-called 'republican' and 'socialist' era when slogans of liberty and freedom were commonplace, it was changed to a prison used primarily for humiliating intellectuals, politicians, religious scholars and other prominent Iraqis.

On his arrival, Sheik Hamoodi saw that a group of religious scholars and politicians of differing persuasions had just been taken to the Revolutionary Court, which was a special tribunal where there was no appeal, and which was generally known for its harsh rulings. He later learned that members of this group were ordered by this court to be executed. He remained for two years in Al-Fudhaliah, a despicable and dirty place, which was heavily infected by lice. At times, the place would overflow with detainees, so that the prisoners had to sleep outside during the cold of winter. In the midday heat of the long Iraqi summer, they endured the scorching sun. Some contracted diseases as a result of this exposure, such as lung inflammation. The halls and rooms of the prison were divided on the basis of assigning forty-five centimetres for each detainee, irrespective of his size, height or weight. Some resorted to mutual exchanges of places, in order to provide sleeping space for each person at different times. There were only two or three lavatories for every 500 prisoners or more.

Next, Sheik Hamoodi was transferred to another prison. The conditions at Abu-Gharail were awesome. But, in comparison with the two years at Al-Fudhaliah, the new prison seemed like paradise. However, this new-found 'luxury' did not last long, as he was soon returned to Al-Fudhaliah. Finally, in 1978, he achieved freedom on bail, a relative liberty.

He commented that while in jail, it had become clear to him that his future was uncertain, and any worldly expectations had a trivial aura about them. The only hope was in Allah, and in a personal belief that this path was the right one. In prison he could see the lowest of all people dictating to, and abusing, the good and educated. In essence, the only prevailing ideas were brute force, low-mindedness, and prostitution of honour. These formed the basis of all dealings and behaviour on the part of governors, prison wardens and those who co-operated with them.

The arrest and imprisonment proved an eye-opener and a deep experience for him. He had come to realise that within totalitarian regimes, man, whether great or small, was nothing but a line on a page, and this line could easily be crossed by a simple word: 'execution'. It is also possible for this line to be forgotten when rewritten on another page by another brutal prison warder, who are so numerous in lands ruled by despots, so that the hapless individual would continue to be ignored and would rot in some jail, whether over or under the ground.

The jail was, for Sheik Hamoodi, a pivotal, personal trauma. He had come to know that life has no value – however sweet it may be – if there is no supreme aim towards which man is moving. The regime had tried to divert him from his sacred objectives in life, as symbolised by the call for righteousness and for the service of man. They had failed.

In 1979 he had learned that they had decided to arrest him once more – by the same method and from the same venue, but using a larger group of security personnel. He therefore had no choice but to flee to save his skin and make himself inconspicuous for several months, and then to migrate.

He added: 'My heart falls for you, those who enter Saddam's detention centres . . . may God give you strength when you are tortured . . . when the honour of your families is transgressed upon in front of your eyes . . . when you are subjected to electrical shocks . . . when your eyes are pulled out . . . when your limbs are cut off with a saw . . . and . . . when . . . '

Our meeting finished, I went on to the house of Dr Ramadan, an old and valued friend and the head of the main office of the Ayatollah. He wanted me to meet his wife, a beautiful woman, very quiet and with a lovely smile. Settling down in their house, surrounded by gifts of fruit, biscuits and cakes, and offered but rejected mutton stew, I asked her to tell me her tale. She was known as Mother of the Martyrs because almost her entire family had been taken away. Killed, imprisoned, tortured, or just removed for ever and never heard about again, some thirty-six of her immediate family members had been extinguished by Saddam Hussein. Her first husband was only a primary schoolteacher. His crime? He was a worshipper of God. Not even a mullah, or a sayyid, nor yet an ayatollah, he was just a layman who prayed regularly. As a primary schoolteacher under Saddam Hussein this was a crime against the State. Chased, tortured, beaten, he still went on. In order that he should not see his family they sent him to primary schools many miles outside the city centre. For twenty-five years he taught in different primary schools, barely coming back to see his wife.

They did not have the money to travel. Subsequently, and when he finished teaching, he was captured. Seven months later they returned his body, hardly recognisable, with both eyes taken out, with marks of beatings and long tortures scarring almost all his corpse. The scars were old and some had partially healed. It was clear that from the day he had been taken, he had been tortured relentlessly.

The two children she had left came in to see me, too, a boy and girl. In their late teens they were all that remained of a happy family photograph they showed me, smiling and excited children of ten, eleven, twelve and thirteen, with their loving father and mother. Gone, with pain-filled deaths, and his widow now married to Dr Ramadan, who had been given a house by the Iranian Government, and who honoured the outstanding martyrs of the Saddam Hussein regime by looking after those remaining. And yet she smiled and laughed from time to time, behind the veil of sorrow still yet recognising love and laughter. The schedule of her family losses is below.

On the way back to the place where we were staying, I asked my companion for the first time about his own story. Dr Al-Bayati had been tortured too. He regarded himself enormously fortunate in that he had been arrested very early on in the reign of terror, which started when Saddam Hussein took over in 1979, and although he had been very severely beaten, in his terms he had got away lightly. He only had a permanently damaged back which meant that he could barely lift a briefcase. He thought himself most fortunate. British surgeons had looked several times at the possibility of operating but said the risk of total paralysis was just too great.

I found these stories simply horrific. But they had to be heard and interwoven with aid work and my political effort came the thread of publicity. The ITN crew from Belfast who came to the marshes with me in October

Mrs Om-Jalal's Family

Serial No.	Names & Family Name	Birthday	City	Relationship	Personal Status
1.	Mohammed Badai es-Salim		Basra	Her spouse	Martyred in 1979
2.	Jabir Mohammed B. es-Salim	1966	"	Her son	Detained in 1981
3.	Jaafer M. Badai es-Salim	1967	"	" "	Detained in 1982
4.	Wafaa M.B. es-Salim	1960	"	Her daughter	Detained in 1982
5.	Hiafao H.B. es-Salim	1961	"	" "	Detained in 1962
6.	Hassan Mohammed Hassan	1955	"	Wafaa's spouse	Detained in 1982
7.	Moukhlus M. Hassan		"	Hassan's brother	
8.	Mujahid H. Hassan		"	Wafaa's brother-in-law	
9.	Moushir Badai es-Salim	1933	"	Family man's brother	Detained in 1982
10.	Hashimiyya Moushir	1952	"	Moushir's daughter	Detained in 1982
11.	Rajaa Moushir	1953	"	" "	Detained in 1982
12.	Ali Moushir		"	Moushir's son	Detained in 1982
13.	Moushin Moushir		"	" "	Detained in 1982
14.	Abdul-Rahman B. es-Salim		"	Family man's brother	Detained in 1979
15.	Ali Sabri al-Zubeidi		"	Mrs Om-Jalal's nephew	Martyred in 1979
16.	Khaddoun Adrean S.S. al-Zubeidi		"	" "	Martyred in 1979
17.	Karim Moushin al Zubeidi		"	" "	Martyred in 1979
18.	Mouzan al-Nasir		"	Mohammed Badai's cousin	Detained in 1982
19.	Wasila Dghiam		"	Mouzan's wife	Detained in 1982
20.	Fatima Mouzan		"	Mouzan's daughter	Detained in 1982
21.	Zianab Mouzan		"	" "	Martyred in 1982
22.	Hussein Mouzan		"	" son	Martyred in 1982
23.	Ali Mouzan		"	" "	Detained in 1982

Serial No.	Names & Family Name	Birthday	City	Relationship	Personal Status
24.	Haiyawi Selman			Family man's cousin	Martyred in 1987
25.	Jassim Hannoun			"	Martyred in 1987
26.	Hassan Talib			Kinsman	Martyred in 1980
27.	Mohammed Abdul-Zahra al-Hir	1957		"	Detained in 1982

Mr Abou-Ahmed Ramadan's Family
(her second husband)

Serial No.	Names & Family Name	Birthday	City	Relationship	Personal Status
1.	Ghazi Ramadan	1940	Amara	Abou-Ahmed's brother	Martyred in 1992
2.	Salih Ramadan	1945	"	"	Detained in 1982
3.	Sabih Dawoud	1950	"	Abou-Ahmed's brother-in-law	Detained in 1981

1991, used their material scrupulously and to good effect. But the lack of follow-up on the ground meant that the issue faded fast. Amar's face helped to revive it with an appeal in *The Sunday Times*, but more material was still needed.

A BBC South and East television team, with a World Service radio reporter and *Sunday Times* photographer, Bob Collier, came on the February 1992 trip to try to visit the south of Iran and bring the refugees' plight to world attention. The weather was against us and, as Iraqi cross-border air-raids were frequent, our small Iran Air aircraft was dependent upon the right wind for coming in to land without straying over dangerous territory. We spent long hours at Tehran airport but could not take off for the south. I managed some business there with the Deputy Head of State (we had a long discussion about the comparison of Islamic and Christian fundamentalism) and with the Minister of Health. He bowed gracefully to my request for free hospital space and operating theatres for severely wounded Iraqi victims. As a result, Guy's Hospital's senior consultant, surgeon Tony Rowsell (by then an Amar Appeal Trustee) accompanied me on a trip six weeks later over the May Day holiday weekend to scrutinise professionally the plastic surgery work of Iranian colleagues. He judged it to be world class, and started our new link between Guy's and Al-Fatimeh Hospital, offering a visiting fellowship.

Four weeks after that, when Christian Whitsun happened to coincide with the annual Mecca pilgrimage of hadj, I took Tony Rowsell back to Tehran with two more Guy's surgeons (John Clarke, the world-renowned expert on childhood burns, and Senior Registrar David Gateley), together with two senior surgeons seconded from Moscow through the kind and efficient work of Vladimir Ivanov, Commercial Attaché of the Russian Embassy to the UK. This eminent East–West humanitarian team assessed 290 patients with a wide variety of wounds and operated upon ten plastic surgery patients. While they were working I travelled south to the camps to assess and report on the now growing work of the Amar Appeal and of the Iraqi Humanitarian Relief Committee (my other commitment).

By this time the dangers in the marshes that week were very great and I managed only a brief trip. The fear of discovery meant that the group of marsh refugees due to meet me disappeared before I arrived, leaving bent reeds to indicate that they had been and gone. The marsh Arab boatmen and mujahedin guards spoke frankly of their concerns at sailing in daylight. The patch of water where we entered was said to have been bombed chemically from the air the previous afternoon. Andrew Hogg, the journalist with me, was just able to fill half a back page of *The Sunday Times* the following Sunday and had no space to mention the surgeons' extraordinary selflessness or the continuing sufferings in the camps. The war story was the only news point found to be of sufficient interest to their wide readership.

In London, in June 1992, I saw the British Foreign Secretary, Douglas Hurd, for a crucial and lengthy briefing meeting. I shared with him all my knowledge and my deep concerns for the fate of southern Iraq. A few weeks later, in July, I formed an All-Party Parliamentary Group for the Iraqi Shi'ites, with knowledgeable and heavyweight Conservative back-bench colleagues such as Tim Rathbone, Sir Geoffrey Pattie and Bowen Wells. The Labour Opposition gave outstanding people too. We put down a stream of Parliamentary Questions just as the House rose for its summer recess. Douglas Hurd then met with James Baker, the American Secretary of State, in the Philippines and raised my concerns.

A month later, I sat at a desk in Indonesia writing an article on the Mad'an for the *International Herald Tribune*'s Singapore Editor, which was subsequently published world-wide. A telephone call from the thoughtful and very competent Minister for Overseas Aid, Lynda Chalker, told me that an air blockade by the Allies

(France, UK and the USA) had been put in place south of the 32nd parallel. I telephoned and faxed southern Iraq and the marshes at once. Beleaguered friends there begged for ground troops too.

The effects on the Shi'ites, particularly in the marshes, because of Saddam Hussein's reaction to the three public humiliations that he had suffered internationally during the summer, was harsh indeed. First, Saddam Hussein had suffered from the free and fair Kurdish northern Iraq elections. A local government, free to operate through Western intervention and the Allied military supporting framework, was in position and had been operative since June 1992. A second blow had come the previous month when the long-awaited UN report on the causes of the Iran–Iraq War had been published. In this the instigator was named and blamed: it was Iraq, under the rule of Saddam Hussein. These two humiliations, I heard from a brother of a former, recently murdered officer member of his Guards, had resulted in an offer being made to Saddam by his generals – to deliver the south to him in chains. They would wipe out the Shi'ites as his birthday present. And finally came the Western air blockade of the south of Iraq. Saddam's engineers rapidly created the way for the Army generals to fulfil their task. The noose around the marshes was starting to tighten.

Because of my difficulty in making a prolonged tour of the marshes, I met some witnesses by prior agreement near the border of Iran and Iraq. Some had come out of the marshes to give me their testimonies, others had escaped badly wounded to seek medical treatment in the safety of Iran. One witness came across the border from Al Amārah with injuries sustained on 16 September near Al-Arga village. The attack had been launched by Saddam Hussein's Army on the marsh villages, with artillery followed by more than 30 tanks with machine-guns and then 30 to 40 boats each carrying 10 armed men. Whole families had been captured, women and children killed.

There were three Divisions of soldiers (20,000 in all) and the local population who were attacked numbered about 25,000 from the following towns and villages: Al Sahain, Al Satuha, Al Abeq, Abotsunha, Al Shede, Slain, Al Kbah, Al Salgel. I list them all so that no one can be in any doubt that they really exist. Since many of these villages are between the Basra highway and the Army front line on the Iranian border, most people had been trapped and killed or captured and removed.

A second witness was a marked man, whose picture was displayed all over Iraq. The price on his head was one car and 50,000 dinars. He became a fighter and leader of a group during the uprising in late February 1991. His motive for joining the uprising was to fight for a free Iraq, against the dictator. He came over the border for the first time ever to explain the situation and the need for urgent action by the West. He reported that:

There is true famine in the marshes. Within two weeks if no urgent action is taken all the people in the marshes will be destroyed. The marshes and artillery assaults ('bombing') in the area is very heavy. Action needs to be quick. The military action in the last four weeks since the no-fly zone was imposed has encompassed: artillery – the Special Guards have all moved to the marshes; the Adran Force – totalling 60 factions [sic] of 120,000 men [i.e. he believed that half of Saddam's ground-based forces were in the marshes]. Many thousands of people have been killed or captured in the last four weeks, e.g. the city of Madaina, where 6,000 people were captured out of a city of 40,000. There will be mass starvation within three months at the outside.

A third man was in acute pain. His wounds were to the bone (he took off his bloody bandages in agony to show me the hurt). Half of his left hand was blown off. The hand had been dressed in Ahwāz hospital on his

arrival there two days earlier. He was a rice farmer
whose farm had been burned down. He reported that his
family came from Al-aggia and had always lived in the
marshes. The 250 village houses were of reed, on stilts
in the water. Twelve days before (9 September 1992) his
village and nearby villages had sustained heavy artillery
bombardment. Most of the houses were destroyed and
some families were killed then or in the subsequent
assault by troops. There were, and still are at the time
of writing, continuing daily and even nightly attacks. The
bombardment was extremely heavy before the no-fly zone
and afterwards very severe indeed. The air exclusion zone
stopped aircraft bombing but left the ground attacks. He
said that it had been hard to travel to the nearby town,
Al Addil, to get supplies. All village farms had been burnt
and although there was still a little black-market food in
the towns, with the army blockade it was not possible
to move out of the villages and it was impossible to get
into the towns. Schooling had been unavailable for ten
years, and also medical care, both of which went with the
Iran–Iraq War.

Another witness, a middle-aged man, was born in the
marshes in a village near Al Amārah. Interviewed in the
marshes, he reported that his village had been destroyed
completely and the supporting rice farms burned and
destroyed by Saddam's forces sixteen months ago. His
wife and children, he believed, were still alive but trapped
behind the lines. He said: 'I go deep into the marshes now
only occasionally and for a special mission (such as to take
in Emma Nicholson) as the danger is now very great. It
has increased since the no-fly zone due to the increase in
ground attacks, with assaults each day from cities around
the marshes used as launch pads for attacks on villages by
the sixth troop with tanks and mobile missile launching.
I and my colleagues (wounded in the uprising) ask why
there is no Western pressure to force withdrawal of the
regime's ground troops below the 32nd parallel?'

Finally, two young men spoke up, one was badly

wounded and traumatised, and reported that six months earlier his home in Chidhi was destroyed and all members of his family were killed. He managed to escape with difficulty and crossed the Iran border. The second one, injured in head and body, not wholly articulate because of head injury, reported that he had arrived in Iran in February 1992. His family's rice farm had been destroyed by artillery bombing, and some family members killed. He believed that his family and their way of life were finished for ever.

I asked them questions I had so often asked before. Given the terror that the regime rules by, what was the position of Saddam Hussein, and why was he still in power? They replied that the Army morale was very, very low, that they were disenchanted with the policies of Saddam Hussein, which made them take unsuccessful risks. They saw no point in confrontation as they could not fight the West and win. The Army were now thinking of the future. They believed that any change of leadership must come from the will of the people.

People had been talking publicly in the last few months against Saddam Hussein, saying that his latest international provocations were undertaken to raise his status in the eyes of the people. The wounded men told me that it was many years since public opposition to Saddam Hussein had been expressed like this. The population dreamt of seeing the end of Saddam Hussein. While he remained in power they saw nothing good happening within Iraq. But there was also criticism of the military action undertaken by the West since the Gulf War, as the destruction of the important targets attacked did nothing to help the suffering people.

Human life, values and human rights have had no sanctuary in Iraq for many years and Saddam Hussein had total sovereignty. He could not live except through creating violence and hatred.

I asked how the security surrounding Saddam Hussein was organised. They told me that the main HQ for Private

Security (Amn Khas) is in the heart of Baghdad, and that the main building complex, the White Palace, is in Al Bataween district but is surrounded by residential and office buildings. It hosts all central command and communications for the security forces. The main areas occupied by Saddam and his private security forces (the Amn Khas) surrounded the Presidential Palace on both sides of the river. The two main areas are from the Babylon Hotel towards Abu Nowas Street and opposite the Presidential Palace. The area hosts Saddam's most trusted élite.

The two young men told me that in the countryside, all main provinces have clearly identified intelligence buildings which function as Saddam's most influential instruments. The buildings are the key in maintaining the communications and command of the above HQ with the provinces. For example, in the Shiah holy city of Najaf, south of the 32nd parallel, the main building for intelligence is easily identified by its location, size and antennae, behind the main province building on the Kufa main road. It can be singled out with no residential buildings nearby. Another example is in the Shiah holy city of Karbala, north of the 32nd parallel, where the main building is also for intelligence and can be recognised on the Baghdad road in the same way.

The way to defeat Saddam Hussein is to destroy his power base so that the Army can rise up against him. But he is apparently impregnable, shielded by forces too great to conquer. He is protected and surrounded by five agencies of terror, who are the pillars of his power. In total these number 150,000 men, each of whom is especially recruited and who are commanded by members of his immediate family. The harshest agency in Amn Khas (Private Security), is headed by his son, Qasa. This has no headquarters building but is located in defined areas on both sides of the river in Baghdad. There are approximately 3,000 men in Private Security (an upper limit of 5,000) of whom 1,000 travel with Saddam when he moves. They create a three-mile radius physically around his movements and man every building. At the same time, three or four other areas are treated in the same way so that his movements are obscured. Their technique lies in stage-managing effects (retinues of twenty Mercedes, for example), and their checking procedures of visitors are too thorough (ears, eyes, lips, hands are medically examined) for an assassination to be likely.

The young men then told me where Saddam's military and intelligence manoeuvres are planned. The main HQ complex for Intelligence (Mukhabarat) is located near the site of Baghdad International Exhibition, a main building with clear antennae which stands far from other residential and/or office buildings. This hosts all central communications for the Intelligence. The main HQ complex for Military Intelligence (Istikbarat) is sited on the shores of the river in Khadimaya, next to the Al Aaema bridge, and it also stands apart from other buildings. It handles all central commands for the Military Intelligence.

The young men ceased talking. Their exhaustion was apparent and their wounds hurting. I left into the night with the Medical Superintendent's parting plea for painkillers and antibiotics ringing in my ears.

In September 1992 I returned once more to Iraq. The new horror story I was told this time was of the drainage of the marshes. It had started in July. The work was vast and stretched throughout the entire wetlands, which was half the size of Switzerland. The Supreme Council, opponents of Saddam, gave me their understanding of the physical changes, derived from marsh-dwellers' reports. It was split into five operations.

The first operation took place in July 1992 in the Maysan province, where the main city is Al Amārah. It apparently consisted of the building of earthen dykes on both sides of the seven main rivers that feed Amārah marshes. These rivers are themselves tributaries of two

larger rivers, Al-Mijar Al Kabir river and Al-Bitaira
river. The effects of the dykes, which were fully built
by the end of July, had been to cut the flow of water
from dozens of small tributaries and streams which
flowed normally out of the seven rivers and irrigated the
land south of Al Amārah city and the marshes beyond.
Four major towns (Al-Maimuna, As-Salam, Al-Adl and
Al-Mijar Al-Kabir, named after the two main rivers) were
without the water on which their continuing existence
depended.

The second engineering operation was completed in
September, while I was in the area. This was the con-
struction of two major earthworks to cut off the estuaries
of all the rivers, tributaries and streams which headed
towards Al Amārah city in the marshes. The two dykes
constructed were 6 metres high, 35 and 25 metres wide
respectively at the base, and 8 metres across the top. The
water of forty rivers was thus being diverted away from
the Amārah marshes to the Euphrates river, many miles
away, to the east and then south.

The third drainage project had been completed in
early July. This was the diversion of the natural and
historic flow of the Euphrates starting from the city
of An Nāsirîyah so that the Euphrates had become a
siphon to take the waters out of Al-Hammar marsh. (The
Euphrates flows south at a lower level than the marsh,
making this operation possible.)

Engineering operation number four consisted of the
building of a 5-metre high dam, 25 metres wide, 6
metres across the top and 7 metres in length, in the
provinces of Nāsirîyah and Basra, along the eastern
bank of the Euphrates to cut off the river's flow into
a group of four rivers that are important water sources
with their tributaries for Al-Hammar marshes. In this
and the following project the Baghdad engineers used
old earthworks erected in the Iran–Iraq War as a basis.

The final project identified was one to dry out an area
of nearly 1,500 square kilometres, by partitioning the

marshes with more dams. These major and potentially irreversible engineering works were being carried out almost secretly. There was no publicity about the projects within Iraq, although four major ministries (Petroleum, Manufacturing and Military Production, Housing and Industry, and Agriculture and Irrigation) were involved in the work which was using up large manpower and other resources. If this were a beneficient policy of land reclamation for agriculture and the voluntary resettlement of a grateful and underprivileged group of indigenous people, surely any Government seeking national and international support would trumpet its progress and achievement?

In fact, the violence employed by the authorities against the inhabitants of the marshes, the use of military force to protect the various work phases, along with the secrecy used to hide it led to the single conclusion that this is a drainage scheme forced on an unwilling people and designed, at best, to control them and, at worst, to obliterate them and their way of life and livelihoods completely.

In the marshes of Iraq, water is the source of life for everything. Drinking water is the first necessity. There are no pipes supplied and, without the waters of the Tigris and the Euphrates flowing through channels and waterways of the marshes, people cannot live there at all. Death by dehydration is the result. Animals, too, will suffer the same fate, particularly the water-buffalo who, as the name suggests, is partially aquatic. Fish cannot survive and hunting will cease. Rice-growing stops without constant irrigation (rice is a southern Iraq and an Iranian staple grain). The economy of this part of Iraq depends upon the flow of water, as does communication and the whole ecology. I felt it must be clear that if the plans were not stopped or altered drastically, hundreds of thousands of men, women and children would either die or have been forcibly removed by the results of drainage, and compelled to change their lifestyles for

ever. More than two-thirds of the marshes had been
drained by summer 1993. The people could not survive.

Date-growing has also been a source of food and earnings for the local people for generations. In the province
of Basra, plantations were said to have been bulldozed
and their water supplies cut off. Destruction of reclaimed
land was also taking place. One-quarter of the cattle in
Amārah province were raised in a 2,000-square-kilometre
grazing area surrounding um Al-Halieb Island. This and
other dry plantation areas were destroyed by bulldozing
the soil from there to build the dykes and dams in
the marshes. Finally, the economic blockage that the
troops had imposed upon the marshes since the no-fly
zone started, prevented the delivery of food and fuel
and forbade marsh people from selling fish or buying
in food.

I saw some of the effects of the drainage on a journey
into the marshes. The water level was down and the reed
roots showed. Few water-buffalo or fish were still alive.
The difference between the marshes as described now and
even thirty-seven years ago is profound.

Lady Alexandra Metcalfe wrote an account of a trip
which she made into the marshes in 1956 in her diary:

There are no banks: just bulrushes and reeds on each
side of the wide swiftly running stream, with channels
wide and narrow diverging off. On ground, a foot or two
above the water level, are clusters of reed huts. Canoes
and biggish boats were being poled up the river.

Kubeish is a biggish village. It is proud of its modern
appearance as you land, but luckily this is only a narrow façade, consisting of a promenade and a few offices
at each end and, behind the network of waterways
threading in and out of the islands, one finds the real
village of reed huts and palm trees. I said I wanted to
go in a canoe, so the sheik, who had met me with the
mayor, produced his, with rugs and cushions. We were
poled through the village. The grand canoes are old war

ones – narrow and thin with lovely upward-curving, painted prow and big, flat, metal nails holding the planks together. The twisting waterways are carpeted with a little white flower, ranunculus. On each side, on what there is of dry land amongst the date palms, are built every size and shape of reed hut, surrounded by piles of rolled-up mats and munching cows. The big huts are called *mudhifs* and are used only for entertaining guests. They are beautifully construc-ted, entirely of reeds. They are barrel-vaulted and have 7, 9, 11, 13, or 15 arches, varying in length, but the biggest can be 60 feet long and 18 high. The rib of each arch is a circular bundle of 20-foot high reeds, tied together. At the base it is 7 to 9 feet in circumference, tapering to about two feet at the top. Four thick and tapering pillars support the ends (outside) and the barrel roof is covered with layers of matting. Between the pillars at each end is open-work lattice in different designs. Matting is on the floor and, for the entertainment of guests, carpets are thrown down and cushions put round the edge. Coffee is served in the centre. The whole effect is beautiful and rather like a cathedral. When they are newly built, the reeds are gold in colour but as they weather, the outside becomes nutria and the inside goes a pale mahogany. The Marsh Arabs or Ma'dan have lived here for thousands of years, maybe as early as 4000 BC, and their way of life can have changed little. They are self-supporting: a little grain or rice, fish, buffalo meat and dates are their diet, and from the reeds they seem to construct everything else they need.

She brought alive again the picture so familiar to English language readers through Wilfred Thesiger's classic, *The Marsh Arabs*. We knew them well from afar.

And still the drainage continued, with the erection of marsh-based 'Berlin' walls. Would no one listen?

10

Against the Odds

On my return to Britain I found a similar reaction of disbelief to my tales of victims' sufferings as a year earlier. It was the anniversary of my first visit to the marshes and the anniversary of the same unwillingness to listen. Surely this was such a catastrophe that at last the world would act? The planned destruction of our shared biblical and pre-biblical heritage, that vast and lovely water-and-reed wilderness, all would be gone without any sound.

My trip had only been for four days (working round the clock) and my return was hasty in order to join a debate in Parliament on the new deployment of the British Armed Forces in Iraq (air cover) and Bosnia. I made another speech in the Commons. Douglas Hurd listened quietly and understood, as did the Foreign Office officials. But others did not seem to grasp the significance of the marsh destruction; it was still too far away and the time for minding about Iraq was past.

One Member, George Galloway, followed my marsh drainage speech by commenting that the loss of some drinking water for Arabs was not an important matter. The West had moved on to Bosnia, and Somalia and Sudan were also high up on the public menu for disaster feasts too.

My frustration was one that all who grapple with human need share: the public only seem to be able to hold

in their mind one problem of pressing importance, and
then only for a short period. However, we walk by faith
and not by sight and six weeks later, four friends from
Tehran arrived in London with no notice. Dr Ramadan,
Sayed al Jazaeri and Mr Shaerastani, accompanied by
a merchant member of our EC aid team, came to show
me maps their men had just captured in the marshes
from the senior water engineer of the Saddam Hussein
regime. They gave the results of his professional work and
offered me a new avenue to explore. Here was the visual,
mapped proof that I needed of dams in the marshes, of
built-up dykes and drying farms and villages. I took the
group straight to the Foreign Office and then acted upon
a suggestion put to me earlier by Rend Rahim of the Iraq
Foundation in Washington that I address the Security
Council of the UN in New York.

I went to New York on Friday, 18 December 1992
for just twenty-four hours, wondering if the Security
Council members would really be willing to learn from
my experiences. In the tall, United Nations building,
the meeting was hosted by two non-aligned members
of the United Nations – Venezuela and Hungary, whose
Ambassadors were both in the chair. Four permanent
members of the Security Council came (France, Russia,
UK and USA) and five other countries were represented
from the non-permanent, rotating membership (Japan,
India, Pakistan, Djibouti and Brazil). The meeting lasted
from 10.30 a.m. until 1 p.m. Two senior staff members of
the British Mission to the UN helped with the video-tape
displays and map backdrops. Each member was given
a package of materials, put together by my secretary,
copied at short notice by Dr Al-Bayati and his colleagues
at the office of the Supreme Council for Islamic Revolution in Iraq, which is based in London, and collated in
our hotel rooms by my hosts, Rend Rahim Francke and
Mahdi Al-Bassam of the Iraq Foundation.

The meeting was successful in so much as it added
to the knowledge of those present and was accepted as

an unbiased and accurate statement of personal testimony. The USA delegation's questions were particularly detailed. Other members took the knowledge and the material as an affirmation of the accuracy of the UN's Special Rapporteur's report (Mr Van der Stoel). This had earlier been seen to have been biased by input from the USA. A number of members spoke privately and informally before and after the meeting, comparing my statements and papers with their own understanding of the situation. Perhaps one or two important perceptions were altered as a result of these discussions, but little was achieved.

It is worth noting that the morning of our meeting was unexpectedly busy for all members of the United Nations, and in particular, members of the Security Council, since the Palestine situation had blown up together with the discovery of bombs in the third consignment of UN Aid to Iraq. The Bosnian no-fly zone and the Somali famine were also on the agenda for this last day of UN work before Christmas. So the size and outreach of the Iraq marshes meeting should not be underrated in the face of these heavy claims on Security Council members' time. I turned to *The Observer* for new media help.

My frustrations were growing again and I turned next to Mr Jan Eliasson, the Deputy Secretary General of the UN Humanitarian Division – the newly created part of the United Nations set up to deal with tragedies such as Iraq. I sought his help urgently for the people trapped in the marshes. We spoke on the telephone and the Head of his Iraq Unit in Geneva, the thoughtful and clear-sighted Dutchman, Gerard Putnam Cramer, came to meet with me for a full day in the House of Commons.

I saw Jan Eliasson in New York for two fierce hours in March. 'What passion and compassion,' he murmured at the end of the meeting, while adding on more reasons why the UN could not do anything at all to help in the marshes. He clearly would not be providing guards or monitors because of the danger. Realistically, there could be no aid delivered if Iraq did not permit free movement for UN officials. I felt as if I was up against a brick wall. I know that many others working for basic justice have felt the same way. Even Christ himself experienced disappointment.

A long meeting in early April 1993 in the Pugin Room of the House of Commons with James Grant, Executive Director of UNICEF, covered the same ground more thoughtfully still. Thirty civil wars were going on, he said, and 33,000 children were dying each day in peaceful surroundings in the developing nations through preventable diseases or causes such as dehydration. These were his priorities. He had no resources with which to help the marsh-trapped Iraqi Shi'ites. He saw no stirring of public opinion to motivate and mobilise the Security Council governments to act either.

The events of early 1993, when the Allies bombed Baghdad in response to Saddam's violation of the air spaces south of the 32nd parallel, did little to help the marsh Arabs. I had a cordial exchange of letters with the Prime Minister, John Major, in which I pointed out that more direct action was needed to help these severely oppressed people. He was supportive, but their suffering continues. With this mixed response I decided to go back to the region in February 1993 to gather more evidence. This was my tenth visit, but it is essential to be stubbornly persistent when you believe in a human cause.

My trip this time coincided with the anniversary of the Revolution of 1979. The city of Tehran, white in daytime with deep snow and bright at night with intricate, Persian-knot designs of light, was celebrating. Over a hundred Western journalists had received visas to visit Iran to see the events. Many of them were dismayed on their arrival to find that visas to Tehran give no authority to travel further, still less to the south.

Shyam Bhatia of *The Observer* – there as a member of my team – slipped quietly into Iraq on a ten-day voyage of discovery. A brave and delightful man, there after long discussions I had held before Christmas with his editor, the thoughtful David Randall. Shyam spoke Arabic and merged into the Iraqi landscape. His five-page report, photographs and video material were shown world-wide. He wrote graphically of the terrors and daily destruction of life and property by Saddam Hussein's attacking forces in the marshes. His work was denounced at once by a Baghdad spokesman. It was a testimony to a vanishing people. *The Observer* ran a continuing appeal for humanitarian aid to be spent in memory of Farzad Bazoft by the Amar Appeal. (Farzad, their journalist, was executed by Saddam Hussein.) *Observer* staff memories are long.

A quartet of small reports were published around that time. The difficulties of access meant that there was little, if any, fresh material displayed in them as the authors could not visit the marshes. But they made clear, helpful statements of the deteriorating situation. The Minority Rights Group, in part triggered by myself, commissioned former Oxfam water engineer Catherine Johnson to do a mini report. She had worked in Basra some time before on water supplies. Barbara Stapleton managed to visit Iran and her report was published by the All-Party Parliamentary Human Rights Group. *Middle East Watch* editor, Andrew Whitely, also reached the camps in Khozestaan, south-west Iran. He had seemed somewhat dismissive of Shi'ite concerns in earlier correspondence and at a meeting did not respond to the evidence. But his five-day stay in Ahwāz gave him the face-to-face evidence from refugees that he sought for his conversion to the truths they had been saying for so long. Amnesty subsequently ran a large advertisement in *The Observer* at Easter, using the marsh Arabs as an example of the need for their work.

But timing is crucial in politics − and the situation was a political matter. Bosnia had taken up available compassion time and space in the media. Few people are knowledgeable enough to respond to disasters without mass picture coverage. In any case, why did the organisations not believe the victims earlier? I don't think I am being over critical here. In this case ignorance is not a defence. There has been plenty of evidence around from refugees in the West; and letters, telephone calls and faxes too. I believe it was symptomatic of the West's collective unwillingness to listen.

Of course, throughout the many months of work undertaken to bring the plight of the Iraqi victims to the attention of the international public, and especially the world's leaders, there have always been individuals who have been prepared to listen. When appeals have needed to be organised or delivery work undertaken, I have been continually humbled by those ready and willing to offer practical and selfless help. I feel sure that others can follow their example.

One additional way of contributing to a cause is to bring pressure to bear on those in a position to influence change on a wider scale. This requires imagination and determination, but I am confident that it can be successful if enough people join with you. As a Member of Parliament I can testify that the concerns of the electorate do make politicians sit up and take notice. We are by no means impervious to intelligent campaigning and that is how I first took up the cause of the marsh Arabs.

On the last day of the 1993 winter session of the House of Commons – Friday, 2 April – I was given the first adjournment debate by Madam Speaker to talk about Iraq. We started our sitting, as we always do, with prayers. As I said the Lord's Prayer on that morning, our plea to God to 'deliver us from evil' took hold of my heart. We were seeking help for ourselves, but, as it appeared to me, we seemed content to allow evil to be visited on others away from our safe haven.

The Lord's Prayer reminded me of the cry from the lips of the Shi'ites, which comes from the Koran transcribed 1,500 years ago: 'He is Allah most gracious: we have believed in Him, and on Him we have put our trust, so

soon will you know which of us it is that is in manifest
error. Say, "See you?" If your stream be some morning
lost . . . who can then supply you with clear flowing
water?'

The House had been kind to me in allowing me time
for debate over the two years during which I had been
working for the people of Iraq, and especially for the
people of southern Iraq and those in the marshes. But
more time for debating their needs was crucial as the
situation had worsened. They had become the forgotten
people, the Ma'dan, the marsh Arabs, and those other
people who were sheltering in those marshes with them.
In all, I estimated that we were discussing about 600,000
people.

This special debate took place in the wake of a first
meeting that the Foreign Secretary and subsequently the
Prime Minister had held on 30 March with a delegation
from the Iraqi National Congress. I was able to put on
record in *Hansard* the crucial points which the INC,
at last fully representative of all the Iraqi Opposition
parties, had raised.

First, they had called for a new United Nations Security
Council resolution to enact Resolution 688, which charges
Saddam Hussein not to wage war on his own people.
Secondly, they had urged the Prime Minister and the
Foreign Secretary to concentrate upon discussing practi-
cal methods of reversing the current repressive measures
instituted by Saddam's regime.

Thirdly, they had sought help for the removal of the
extensive and ecologically destructive activities of the Baghdad regime in the marshes, such as on the dams and
drainage channels. Fourthly, they had sought British
assistance for the removal of the economic blockage
against Iraqi Kurdistan in the north, and especially
the denial of petroleum products, without which people
there could not keep warm or live. They had also asked
for the cessation of arbitrary executions in Baghdad, the
release of all political prisoners and the return of the

hundreds of thousands of Iraqi deportees to their homes throughout Iraq.

They sought the extension of the no-fly zones to include all of Iraq, which was a possible Western action. And, most importantly, for the adoption by the United Nations Security Council of the recommendation of the Special Rapporteur on Human Rights in Iraq to place human rights monitors all over Iraq. In the wake of that, the delegation requested a security zone, a safe haven, in the marshes. Finally, they had asked for a war crimes trial for Saddam Hussein to be mounted.

The Foreign Secretary, the Prime Minister, the Minister of State and the Middle East Foreign Office specialists had given a sympathetic hearing and a large understanding of the many problems outlined by the Iraqi National Congress delegation at the meeting. I stated again in the debate the reasons that lay behind their poignant requests, namely the sufferings of the people in the marshes; the destruction of a wonderful historic part of the world that could never be recreated; and the unwillingness or inability of the United Nations to carry through to logical conclusion their own decisions. I referred to the UN/Baghdad legal tangle, which seemed to prohibit the UN from helping those locked into the marshes by the military blockade and facing probable destruction. I spoke with knowledge, since most days new information comes from the marshes by fax, sometimes by telephone. As the humanitarian work I have been doing has concerned organising medical and food aid, so the medical and nutritional needs of the people in the area are reported fortnightly to the Amar Appeal board by our doctors in SW Iran. I explained to my colleagues that cholera had now started in the marshes – a terrible death, which we have not known in the West for many years. Hardly any food was available because of the blockade by Government forces. Skin and gut infections, diarrhoea, typhoid fever, food poisoning, eye diseases, conjunctivitis, gynaecological and pelvic inflammatory diseases, dental and gum diseases and sunstroke – all these were taking their toll. These diseases are now widespread and largely untreated.

I had been in the marshes where polluted water is now all that there is to drink. Without a place to deposit sewage, either human or animal, most of those now in the marshes suffer constant dysentery. There is no cold chain of refrigeration, and children cannot be immunised. Polio, measles, whooping cough, mumps and other childhood diseases are rampant. The children are stunted as breast milk is in short supply because of severe maternal malnutrition. Without even the most primitive obstetric services, mothers are dying in labour. Prenatal protein deficiency affects a fetus's brain development in the womb.

The effects of Saddam's evil policies have been felt not just by the people living there but also by the environment. The famine has been caused not just by natural factors or a lack of water; we were talking about a planned destruction of a people and of their wonderful environment. Now that the marshes had partially dried out, it had become possible to cause fires by using incendiary bombs. In January, February and March of 1993, telegrams from the marshes to Ayatollah Al-Hakim described villages, people and animals being burnt to death. Rice farms that had supplied the staple diet for the marsh Arabs had been burnt out. The fish had died – a crucial source of protein – and the water-buffalo, which gave milk and meat, had fled because of the bombardments.

This is an historic area. The House of Commons' library contained a book called *Ancient Iraq*, written by Charles Roux and first published in 1964. Updated in 1992, it had been through four reprints. It reminds us of the history of this part of Iraq, going right back to the Sumerians 6,000 years ago. After them came the Akkadians, and the Assyrians, and so we can recall the waters of Babylon, beside which people sat down and wept. Echoes of the

Old Testament of the Bible are to be heard throughout the history of the Iraqi marshes, that unique part of the world where the Tigris and Euphrates have provided the great flow of water that has given people a way of life and the resources on which to found successive civilisations. The Ma'dan pre-date the Arab invasion of Iraq. They are indeed a unique people. Their antique language pre-dates Arabic, and their modern version differs from Iraqi Arabic.

This area contains a great deal of special wildlife. Many people will recall Gavin Maxwell's wonderful book, *Ring of Bright Water*, which was about an otter. Few will recall, however, that the otter, Mijbil, was discovered in and brought back from the marshes of Iraq. It was a unique variety of otter, common in the marsh areas. It is called *Lutrogale Perspicillata Maxwelli*. It was a previously unknown species. The area also contains wild boar, various kinds of terrapin, some rare and threatened species of bird, such as the pygmy cormorant, dalmatian pelicans, marbled teal, red-breasted geese, lesser white-fronted geese, white-tailed and imperial eagles, Bara reed warblers, Iraqi babblers and grey hypercolius. Some of these birds are there all the year round and may be specific to the area.

We should look at the marshes of Iraq as a wetland of unique importance. It is half the size of Switzerland, and it has survived for a long time as an area rich in all kinds of fish, some of which are probably unique to it. The World Conservation Monitoring Centre recently declared the marshes of Iraq as a 'site of primary ecological interest'. But with no apparent possibility of achieving rescue for the marsh people I have recently turned to identifying the destruction of this wonderful environmental area. Not because I had any less concern for the sufferings of the people – the more I visit, the more I learn, the more appalled I am by how harsh their suffering has become, but the world has seemed to react with indifference, saying that these are just another group of suffering people. It is a way to increase the pressure. Perhaps if we ask people to think about the ecological impact, those who write prepackaged letters about the destruction of the rain forest will lend their minds and hearts to the destruction of an area that is replicated nowhere else in the world and seemed to be being physically destroyed now.

Maybe Western imaginations are no longer vivid enough to understand the impact of this drainage on a people's heritage – a drainage so profound and so disgraceful that this land, above water for the first time in history, is becoming completely visible. I learnt first-hand from Bulent Ecevit, the former Turkish Prime Minister, who meets with Saddam Hussein regularly, that Saddam Hussein says the drainage, which he now admits is being carried out, is for agriculture purposes and to benefit the local people. Agriculturalists suggest to me that the land is of such poor quality that it will not sustain any more harvesting, it is not the sort of land that can create the wealth that will feed people. There will be just one meagre harvest and then no more.

In desperation, I have triggered a major survey of the marshes. It is spearheaded by the Chairman of the Wetlands Committee of the International Union for the Conservation of Nature, Dr Edward Maltby of Exeter University. The United Kingdom and most member states of the United Nations are members of the IUCN. Why is the survey so crucial? Because the world needs to see and to examine the evidence for recent changes in hydrology and other environmental conditions in the marshlands complex of southern Iraq. The international community should be made aware of the impact of Saddam's policies on all aspects of conditions in this area through this survey which, although commissioned by the Amar Appeal, is being carried out with scientific impartiality.

The survey will evaluate the likely impact of the changes on the maintenance of the ecological character and environment of the marshes. We need to understand the character of agriculture in the region, and the result of change on human communities within the region, on their food security, the local economy, transport, health and social welfare, culture, education and religions. We have asked the International Union for the Conservation of Nature whether it would conduct the survey under its umbrella.

It seems that ecologists and environmentalists have been watching and waiting for a trigger that would enable them to act. Their concern is shared by us, and it matches the concern of the Amar Appeal friends and supporters about the human aspect of the matter. I hoped that the survey would provide those in authority throughout the world with the material that they might care to use as a trigger for urgent action to stop the destruction of the marshes and of the people in the marshes. But still the people die.

It is not just the starvation and illness, or the lack of water which will result in human and wildlife extinction. Access routes run along the top of the dykes, which means that not only small vehicles but armoured tanks can drive into the heart of the marshes. Saddam Hussein's regime has created the killing fields. The people inside are not armed to defend themselves effectively. The ones whom I have seen on my own trips have only old Russian rifles and a few bullets.

Of course I have enough experience of international aid work and politics to know that the United Nations is the servant of its members, and it is up to us members to decide what we want to do and what pressure we will bring. But there is no shortage of material. The Special Rapporteur for Human Rights in Iraq, the former Foreign Minister of the Netherlands, delivered his latest report on 19 February 1993. It made terrible reading. On 5 March, the UN voted on it and proposed a resolution, which was good. It called for specific and immediate improvements in the treatment of the marsh Arabs. It was adopted by a vote of 46 for, 1 against and 16 abstentions. Again, the UN members stated their deep concern about the grave violations of human rights by the Government of Iraq and said that these have led to a deterioration of the situation of the civilian population in southern Iraq, particularly in the southern marshes.

The UN motion states that the members express their:

> strong condemnation of the massive violations of human rights, of the gravest nature, for which the Government of Iraq is responsible, resulting in an all-pervasive order of repression and oppression which is sustained by broad-based discrimination and widespread terror, in particular:
>
> Summary and arbitrary executions, orchestrated mass executions and mass graves throughout Iraq, extrajudicial killings, including political killings, in particular in the northern region of Iraq, in southern Shiah centres and in the southern marsh areas;
>
> The widespread routine practice of systematic torture in its most cruel forms;
>
> Enforced or involuntary disappearances, routinely practised arbitrary arrests and detentions, including of women, the elderly and children and consistent and routine failure to respect due process and the rule of law;
>
> Suppression of freedom of thought, expression and association and violations of proper rights;
>
> The unwillingness of the Government of Iraq to honour its responsibilities in respect of the economic rights of the population.

The motion goes on and on and on. It requests the Secretary General 'to take the necessary measures in order to send human rights monitors to such locations as would facilitate improved information flows and assessment and would help in the independent verification of reports on the situation of human rights within Iraq.'

Knowledge, knowledge and more knowledge is what we are asked to provide. I have been glad to give the United Nations the knowledge required for an understanding of the needs of people in the marshes. However, while the knowledge emerges, people are dying and no UN aid will be given to the marshes in case that jeopardises the northern aid or creates other political tensions. The toehold in Basra recently achieved by UNICEF is the Deputy Secretary General's sop to Cerberus. The marshes are surely the hell beyond the jaws of that guardian of the dead.

I say to anyone who will listen that Saddam Hussein is a tyrant whose evil is unbelievable. If we fail to help, what right have we to say the Lord's Prayer, to seek delivery from evil for ourselves alone, so readily and happily each day? What special brand of Christianity have we created that insulates us from the evil being done to others? Is evil only to be identified as such if it affects ourselves?

11

Any Answers?

During my long meeting with UNICEF's James Grant
in April 1993, he seemed overburdened with the world's
griefs; and had not the resources to act as he would wish
to act. I thought of the small, crumpled child in Zambia,
squatting and crippled by spina bifida, watching from
the edge of society there. Of the distorted four limbs and
spine of the young man in Malawi's Polio Workshop, and
his delicate sewing and embroidery. He's an unwanted
family member too. I thought of the slight child, slender
with malnourishment, slaving beside her mother in the
fields in south India.

I saw again the child's shoes and little bag among
the millions crammed in glass halls; stripped by her
torturers from this small Belsen victim, stored now next
to the glass cases piled high with the hair of thousands
more. I remembered the book made of parchment, in
Bucharest, Romania, of Jewish children's skin; the soap
cakes distilled from their body fat. And I remembered
Jimmy the idiot, from home, jeered at and sometimes
stoned just because he was not like other children. And
the child-woman in Farnham's Children's Home, another
freak of nature to outsiders.

I saw again the pale mass of human flesh, a head
atop a shapeless body, stump arms to lean on, brief,
makeshift legs, lost beneath the vast body, something on
a rough bedsheet defecating. The huge face splitting into

a shapeless smile with tangible happiness responding to the love of the tired and malnourished Polish nurse, coming to clean up and tidy this child-girl, with an intelligence quota of perhaps ten points. And the intelligent grandmother on the Iran/Iraq border without water, food, clothes or male family members left alive to help her in her task of caring for the remaining grandchildren in a deserted zone.

Why do we forget? Religious intolerance seems to be a large factor in our reaction to Iraq. The Christian half-memory of the Crusades and of the repulsion of the infidels at the gates of Vienna; the Jewish despair in Lebanon. In the West, maybe it is fuelled by the perennial need to have an enemy. Whatever we may believe about other faiths the three great One-God religions at least share the same goal of conquering evil (however defined), either in self or others. We also share in the continuing search for God's love in heaven and earth. Is it too late to recognise these commonalities and use shared strengths to overcome the intolerance of others inherent in us all?

An Englishman said recently, within earshot, about a suffering Iraqi child: 'But they don't feel pain, do they?' They do, my friend, they do; but how can you learn that if you are not willing to be drawn into that child's pain? You don't want that involvement because it would alter you, forcing you to change from a stance of comfortable ignorance to seeing and understanding the needs of others.

Religious intolerance allows us to dismiss others as of less intrinsic value than ourselves, irrespective of their personal qualities or excellence. That is how we manage to forget their suffering. Racial intolerance is an even fiercer version of that blindness if that is possible. For, in extremis, it is possible to alter one's faith; indeed, some people choose to do so and it is their right in every free society to worship or not to worship in the way that they wish. Skin colour or inborn physical characteristics that define an ethnic grouping are for ever unalterable.

To persecute someone for that difference marks out the persecutor indelibly. And yet we allow it to happen; we forget because we mentally dismiss that group as less than human. Josiah Wedgwood's statue of the negro slave bore the text: 'Am I not a man and a brother?' That is the cry that we ignore today and tomorrow and did so yesterday. Skin colour, a different pattern of worship or shape of features; these are the easy excuses we use to turn aside.

Today we blame our personal inactivity for the deprived on everyone but ourselves. 'Charity begins at home', we mutter, not finishing out loud our preferred ending to the sentence, 'and it should end here too.' Or we blame the United Nations, failing to realise that it, too, is made up of people just like us, reflecting our own inadequacies. Perhaps we use national sovereignty as an exclusion mechanism, keeping new influences out as well as people.

Slowly but slowly, new ways of working internationally are emerging. The strains of many disasters may be yet shaping our great agencies (the UN in particular) into becoming the forces for good we yearn to have in charge of difficult decisions which nations cannot take alone. But it isn't easy when we, the public to whom the UN member state governments respond, are still so fickle in our commitment to the poor, the suffering and the dispossessed.

So to those who are hardened to the plight they see on television, I say – don't blame the messengers for your determination not to know the victims, nor to recognise them as people like you and me. Within the confines of our sound-bite culture you only allow a few seconds' half-concentration on a single issue before you deliberately turn your mind away. The sanest, most intelligent people in the media world try hard to tempt you from self-titillation to thoughtful reaction, but with little success. The problem is that you are myself, and that it is my own large weakness which you confront and judge. Forgetfulness is nirvana, the state of bliss. The deepest gift from God to man is memory, which hurts. Memory is both the poisoned chalice and the Holy Grail of our existence. Above the dim lamps in Jerusalem's memorial to the Holocaust dead is engraved a call to recall all victims, everywhere:

VENATATI LAHEM B VEITI UVECHOMOTAI YAD VASHEM TOV MIBANIM UMIBANOT SHEM OLAM ETEN LO ASHER LOH YICARET

Which translates:

And to them I will give in my house and within my walls a place and a name better than sons and daughters – I will give them an everlasting name that shall not be cut off.

But human memory is sterile unless the knowledge recalled is matched with new learning and used to widen the boundaries and stretch the horizons of our understanding. Within that discipline we can discover, as St Bernard did, that 'Life is only for Love, Time is only that we may find God'.

Amar Appeal supporters in the last two years have included:

Alleyn's School, Dulwich; Edgehill College, Bideford; Maynards School, Exeter; The Royal Naval School, Haslemere; Oakham School; St Mary's School, Wantage; Mount House School, Tavistock; The Mall School, Twickenham; Sherborne School for Girls; Hereford Cathedral School; Wycliffe College, Stonehouse; Sedbergh School; Wroxall Abbey School; Coldean Infant School, Brighton; Berkhamstead School; St Albans High School for Girls; King's School, Rochester; Lyndale School, St Albans; Gladstone Road County Junior School, Scarborough; Bedales School; Kingswood School, Bath; Moser's Hall, The Schools, Shrewsbury; Portsmouth Grammar School; Great Waltham C of E Primary School; Tower House School, East Sheen; Warminster School; Wrekin College; Eton College; Stamford High School; Tonbridge School; Felsted School; Rugby School; Marlborough College; Wycombe Abbey School, High Wycombe; Grenville College, Bideford; Brown School, Kelley School and Belleville School, of Newburyport, Massachusetts, USA; and many churches, including St James the Less, Winterbourne.

Sir Philip Harris, Miss U. Milner-White, Mrs Helena Duyck, Miss I.D. Haynes, Mr F. Oliver, Mr P. Glazebrook, Dr S. Haider, Dr M. Aguilina, Miss E.J. McGregor, Dr A.V. Jones, Mr C. Swift, Ms C. Claxton-Vatthauer, Mr M. Walsh, Mrs M.A. Glendenning, Mr & Mrs Lessner, Dr & Mrs R. Thomas, Dr & Mrs Armond, Miss J. Sheridan, Mr J.L. Cusden, Mrs A.M. Brassloff, Mr P.E. Hudis, Ms C. Ker, Mr H. Jones, Mrs E.H. Mackenzie, Mr S. Couldry, Miss B.N. Bell, Sir James Graham, Mr P. Jones, Col S. Ali, Mrs D. Bates, Peritas Limited, Mrs J. Kennedy, Miss N. Samarrai, Mr J. Bennett, Ms R. Pennells, Dr A.K. Shakir, Mr M. Najim, Mr J. Gadelius, Mrs J. Williamson, Kufa Gallery, the INC, the Iraqi Women's Association, Christian Aid, Mrs B. Wheatley, Mr D. Dewes, Devon & Dorset Regt, the Al-Khoei Foundation, CAFOD charity, an anonymous Egyptian benefactor of note, SCIRI, Her Majesty's Government (the Overseas Development Administration), the EC, the Iranian Government, the Kuwaiti Government, Saudi Arabia, Needhams Printers, and others from many countries and from all walks of life.

THE AMAR APPEAL

If you would like to make a donation to help the marsh Arabs of southern Iraq, please make cheques payable to 'The Amar Appeal' and send them to:

> Emma Nicholson, MP
> The House of Commons
> Westminster
> London SW1A 0AA

Your money will be spent on food, medicines or clothing. It will be delivered personally by Amar Appeal medical staff and volunteers to the southern Iraqi children, and families who are in greatest need. All donations will be acknowledged.

THE AMAR APPEAL TRUST OBJECTIVES

'The relief of poverty, distress or suffering by appropriate charitable (whether medical, rehabilitative, financial or other) assistance in any part of the world and in particular (but without prejudice to the generality of the foregoing) by the provision of aid to the needy in Iraq or formerly resident there (including in particular the Iraqi Shia homeless) whether victims (i) of breaches of Human Rights (ii) of any public calamity (including famine, earthquake of pestilence) (iii) of war or civil disturbances (iv) of the immediate or continuing effects of lack of natural or other resources or (v) of any other cause of poverty, distress or suffering.'

Charity number 1007939